Great Street Art
Reggae, Blues, and World Beat Posters, 1977-1989

Victor Burleigh

4880 Lower Valley Road, Atglen, PA 19310 USA

Copyright © 2006 by Victor Burleigh
Library of Congress Card Number: 2005933331

All rights reserved. No part of this work may be reproduced or used in any form or by any means—graphic, electronic, or mechanical, including photocopying or information storage and retrieval systems—without written permission from the publisher.

The scanning, uploading and distribution of this book or any part thereof via the Internet or via any other means without the permission of the publisher is illegal and punishable by law. Please purchase only authorized editions and do not participate in or encourage the electronic piracy of copyrighted materials.

"Schiffer," "Schiffer Publishing Ltd. & Design," and the "Design of pen and ink well" are registered trademarks of Schiffer Publishing Ltd.

Designed by John P. Cheek
Cover design by Bruce Waters
Type set in Korinna BT

ISBN: 0-7643-2271-0
Printed in China

Published by Schiffer Publishing Ltd.
4880 Lower Valley Road
Atglen, PA 19310
Phone: (610) 593-1777; Fax: (610) 593-2002
E-mail: Info@schifferbooks.com

For the largest selection of fine reference books on this and related subjects, please visit our web site at
www.schifferbooks.com
We are always looking for people to write books on new and related subjects. If you have an idea for a book please contact us at the above address.

This book may be purchased from the publisher.
Include $3.95 for shipping.
Please try your bookstore first.
You may write for a free catalog.

In Europe, Schiffer books are distributed by
Bushwood Books
6 Marksbury Ave.
Kew Gardens
Surrey TW9 4JF England
Phone: 44 (0) 20 8392-8585; Fax: 44 (0) 20 8392-9876
E-mail: info@bushwoodbooks.co.uk
Free postage in the U.K., Europe; air mail at cost.

Introduction

Bob Marley died in 1981, but the interest he generated in the reggae, blues, and world beat music grew after his death and continues still. In the 1980s local bands sprang up around the world, and clubs began to feature the music to ever increasing numbers of patrons.

In cosmopolitan cities like New York, Los Angeles, Chicago, and San Francisco young people were attracted to the innovative rhythms and lyrics of the new music. Cutting across cultural and ethnic barriers, they thronged to the clubs, taking their enthusiasm and energy with them.

To advertise these events hundreds of posters were hung on telephone poles, vacant walls, and shop windows. Made on photocopiers and litho presses, by local artists, they have the edge that comes from needing to catch one's attention with a minimum of expense. The result is raw, "in-your-face" street art that captures the spirit of a generation and of the music.

The posters in this book date 1977 to 1989. They were gathered in San Francisco, a city on the cutting edge of the music world and a haven for reggae, blues, and world beat music. Nearly every night one of the many music clubs would offer a live concert of an up-and-coming group. And, since every club produced its own posters, there is a wide variety of styles and graphic images, as well as a history of the music scene captured in these posters.

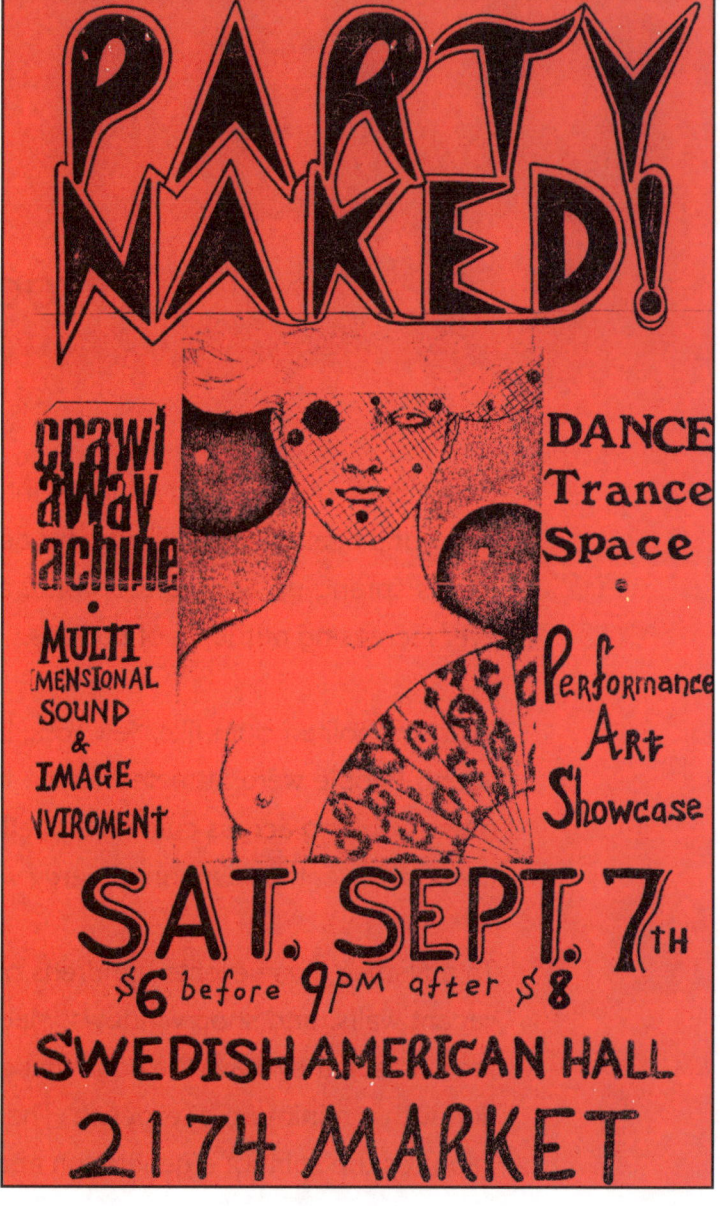

VOICES

w/ VAUXHALL

FRIDAY APRIL 26TH
CHI CHI
440 BROADWAY

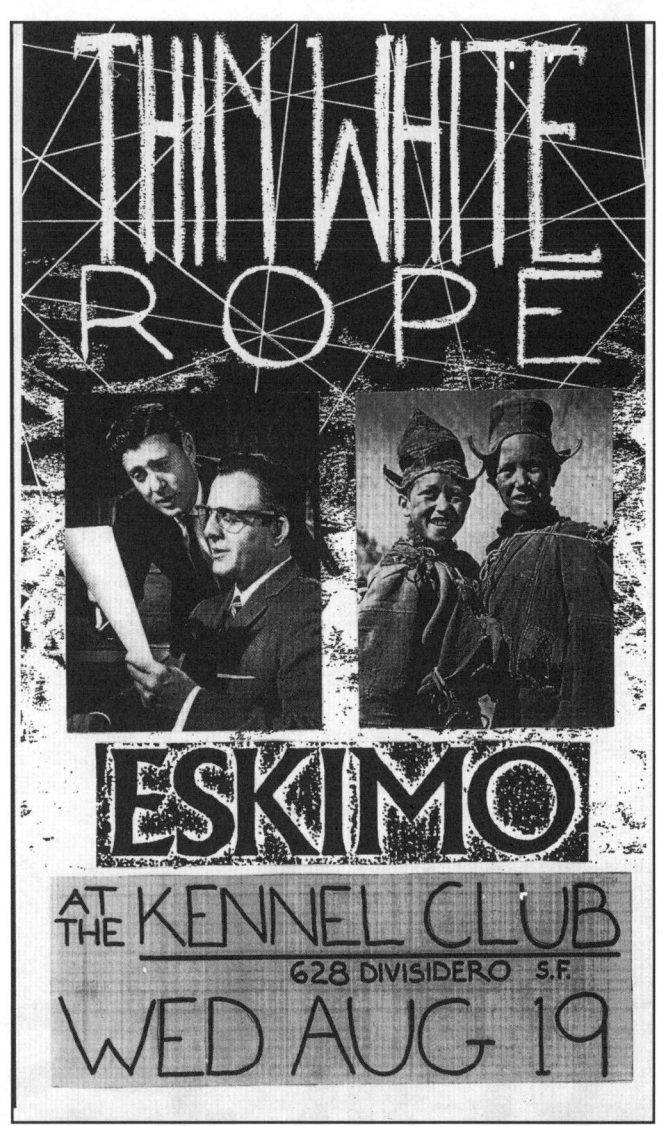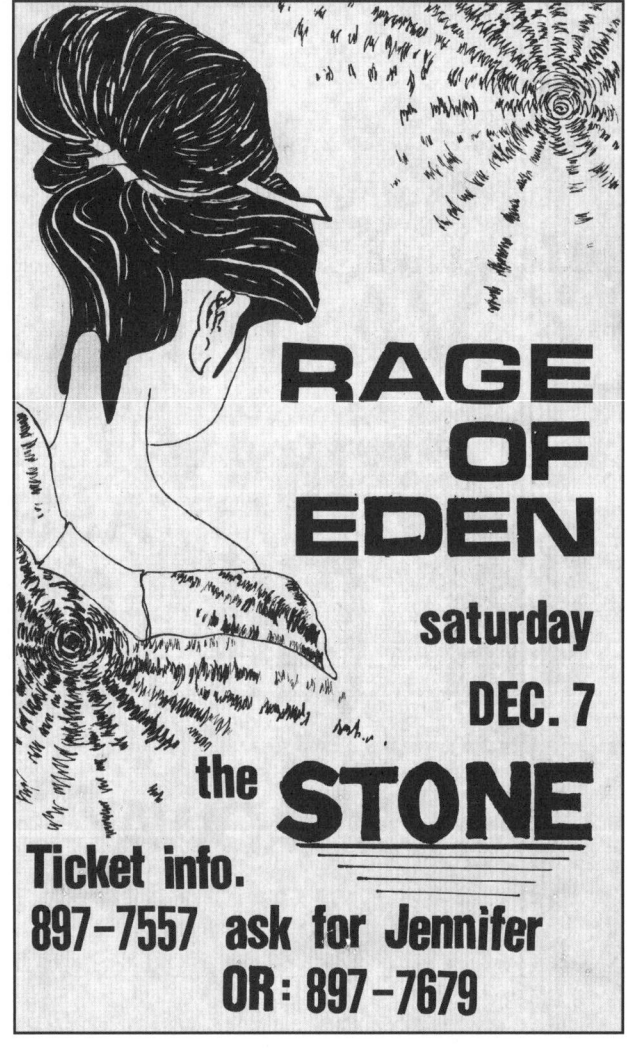

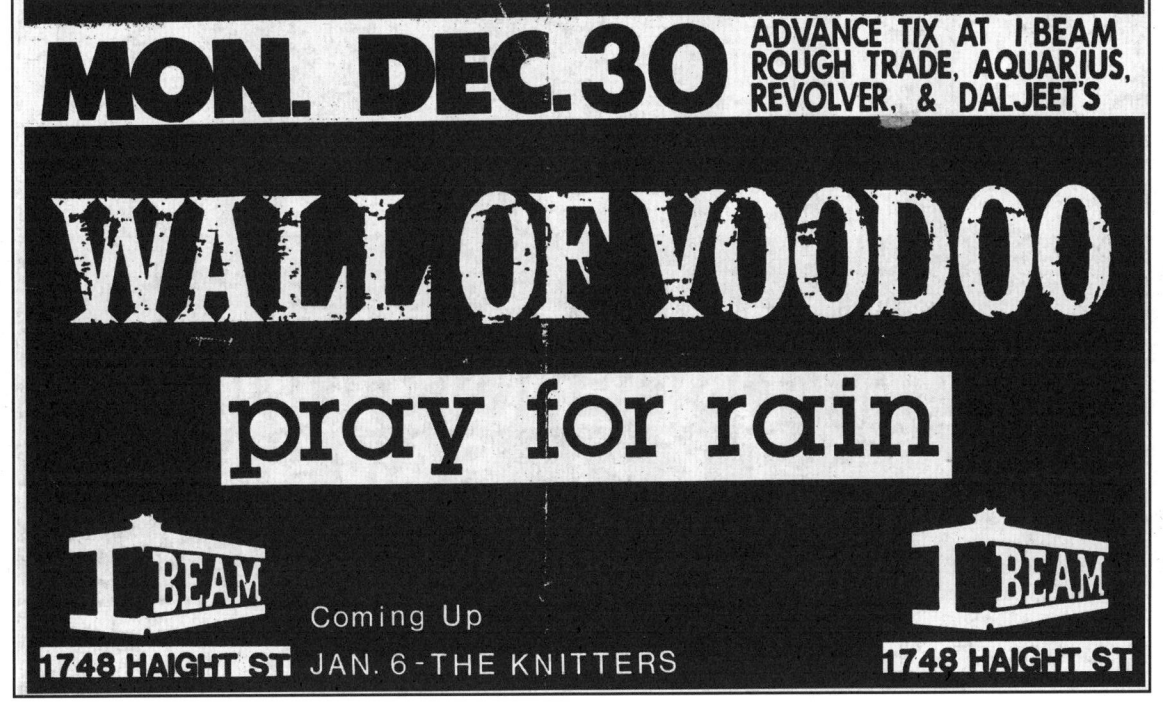

MRS GREEN

11-13 FULL MOON
11-22 UNDERGROUND
11-24 T.K.O. SAN RAFAEL
11-29 RIVER THEATER

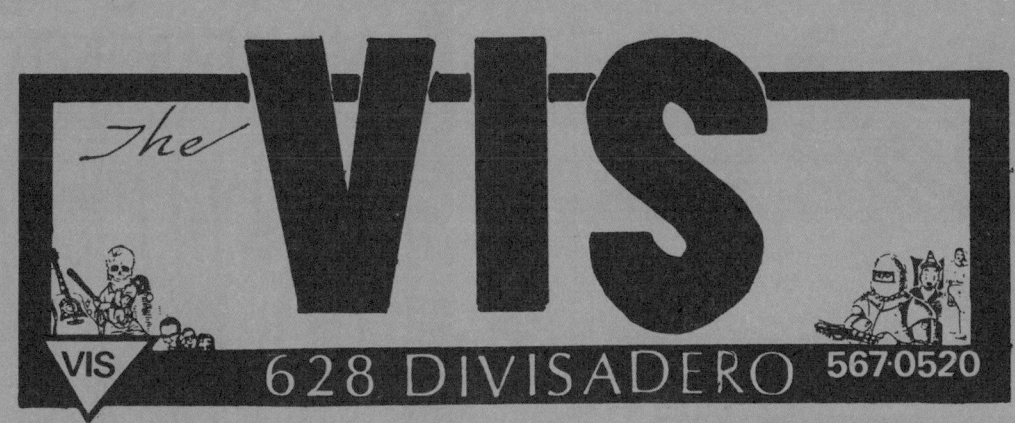

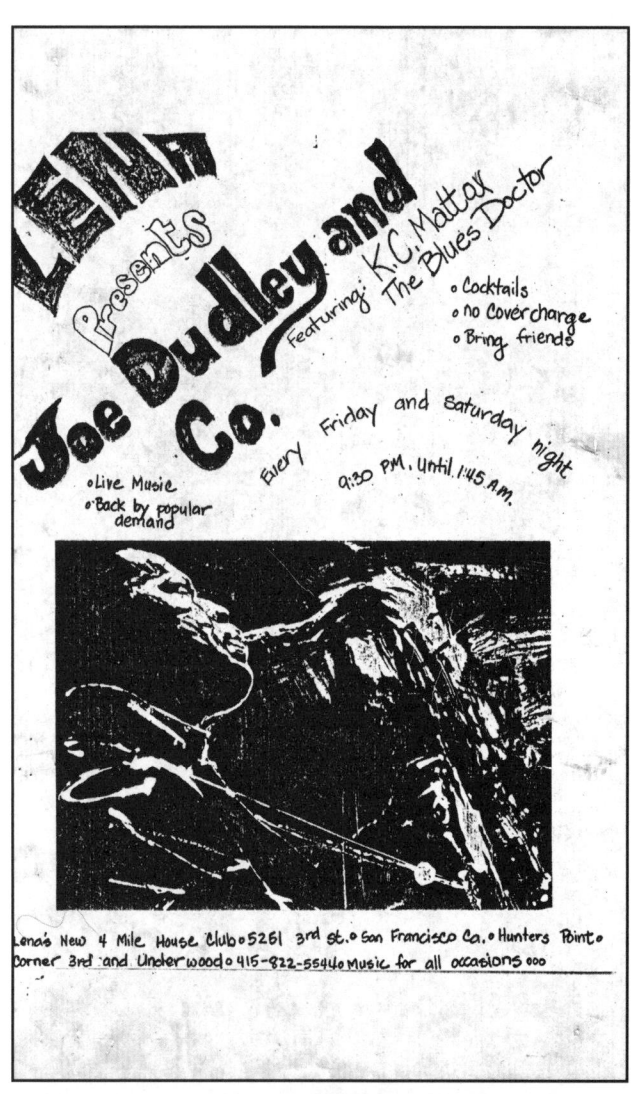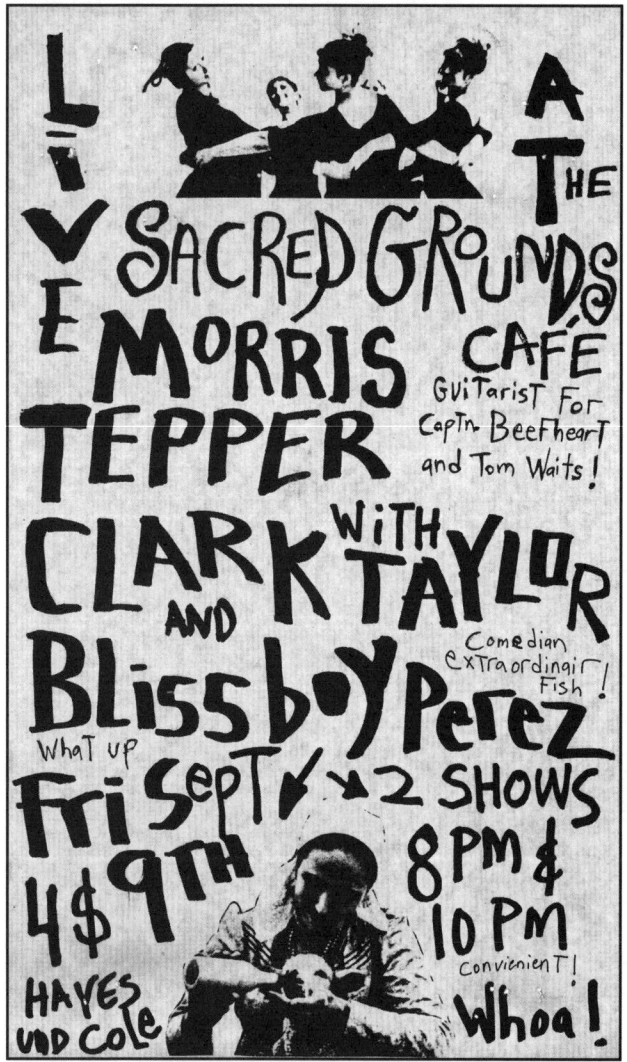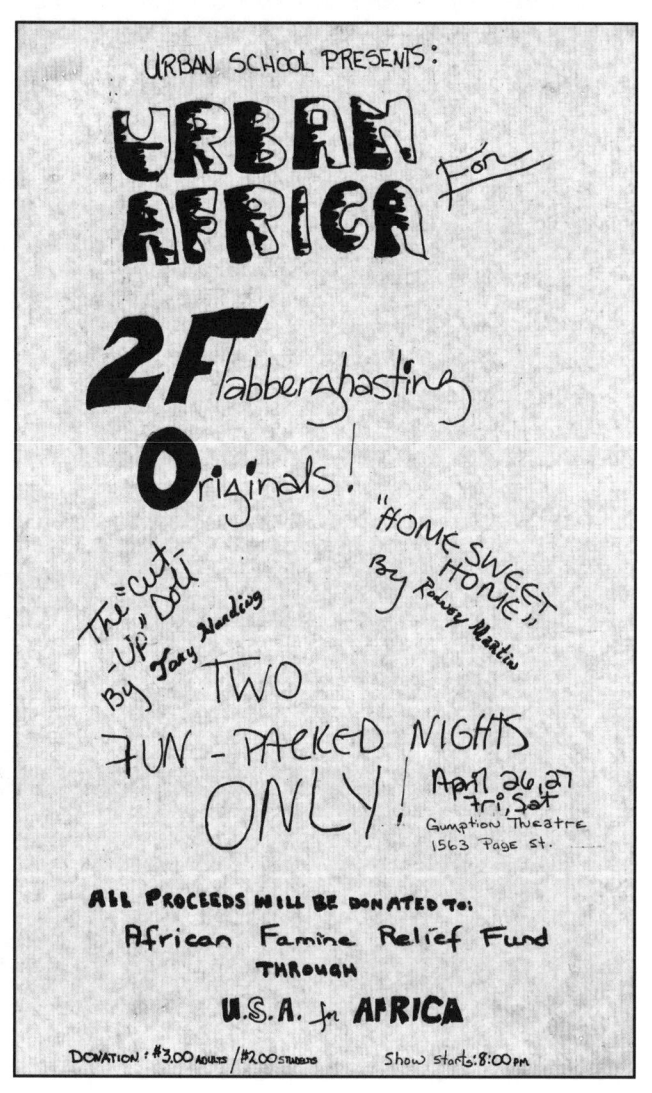

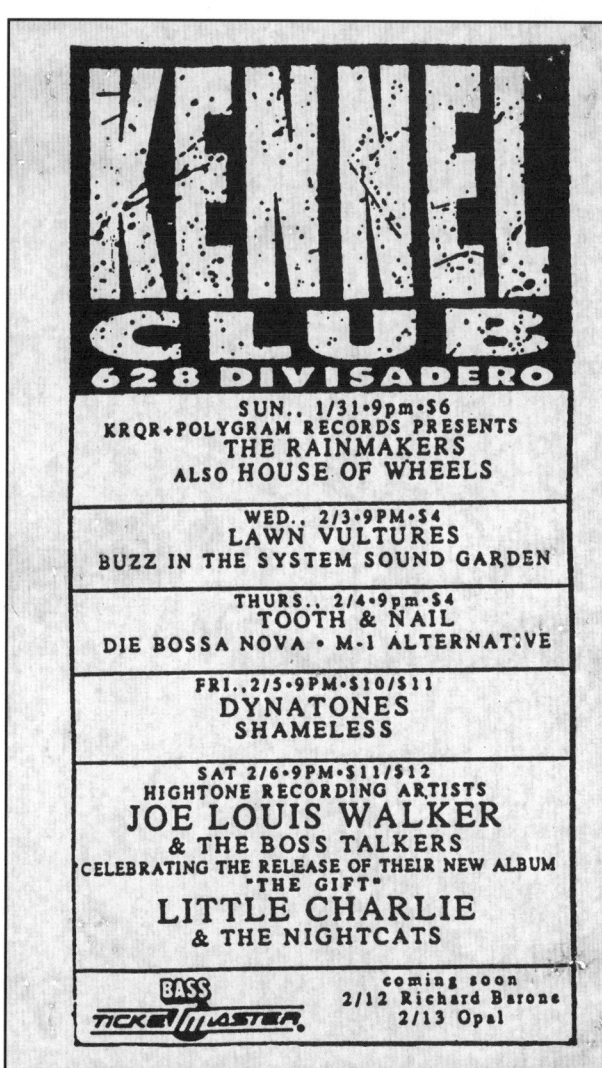

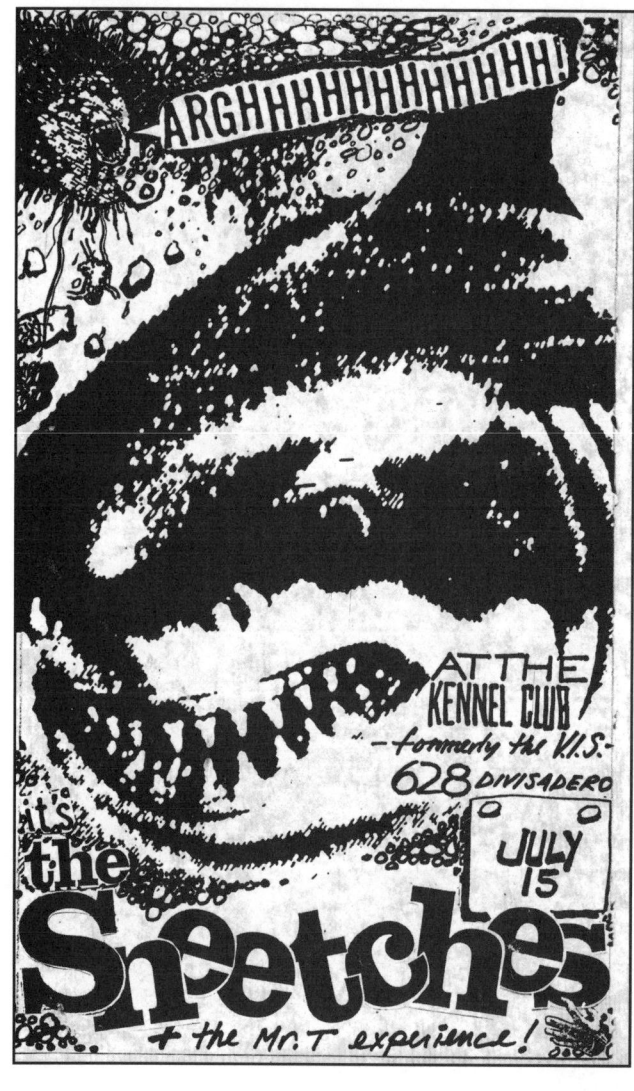

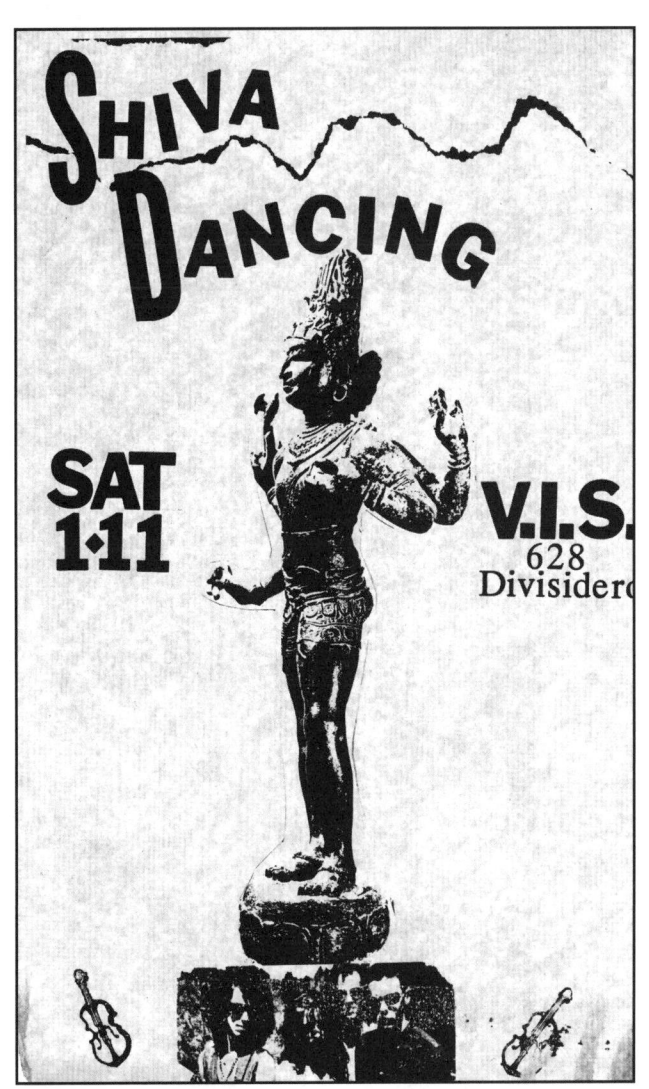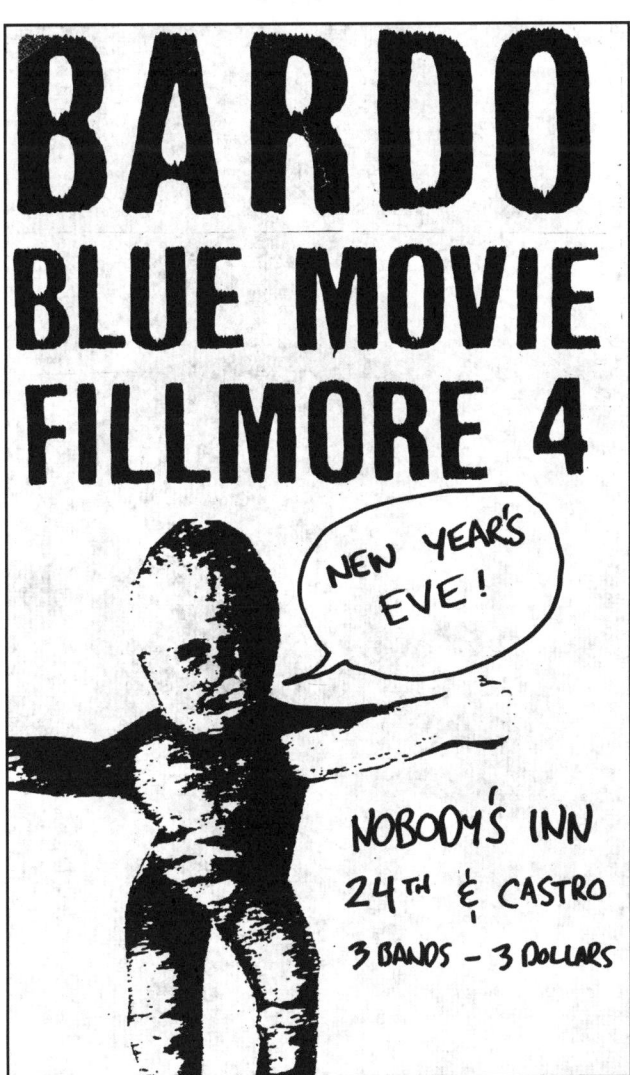

SONIC SURGERY SOUND SYSTEM WITH FUNKEE FRESH POSSEE

FEATURING
RAS SMURFIN', PAPA STRETCH & JAH WIZE

ALSO APPEARING
THE BLACK SWANS
AND
D.J.s SHEA & ESSEN

10PM — **$3**

FIREHOUSE 7 ~ 3160 16TH ST. S.F.

TUESDAY, MARCH 29TH

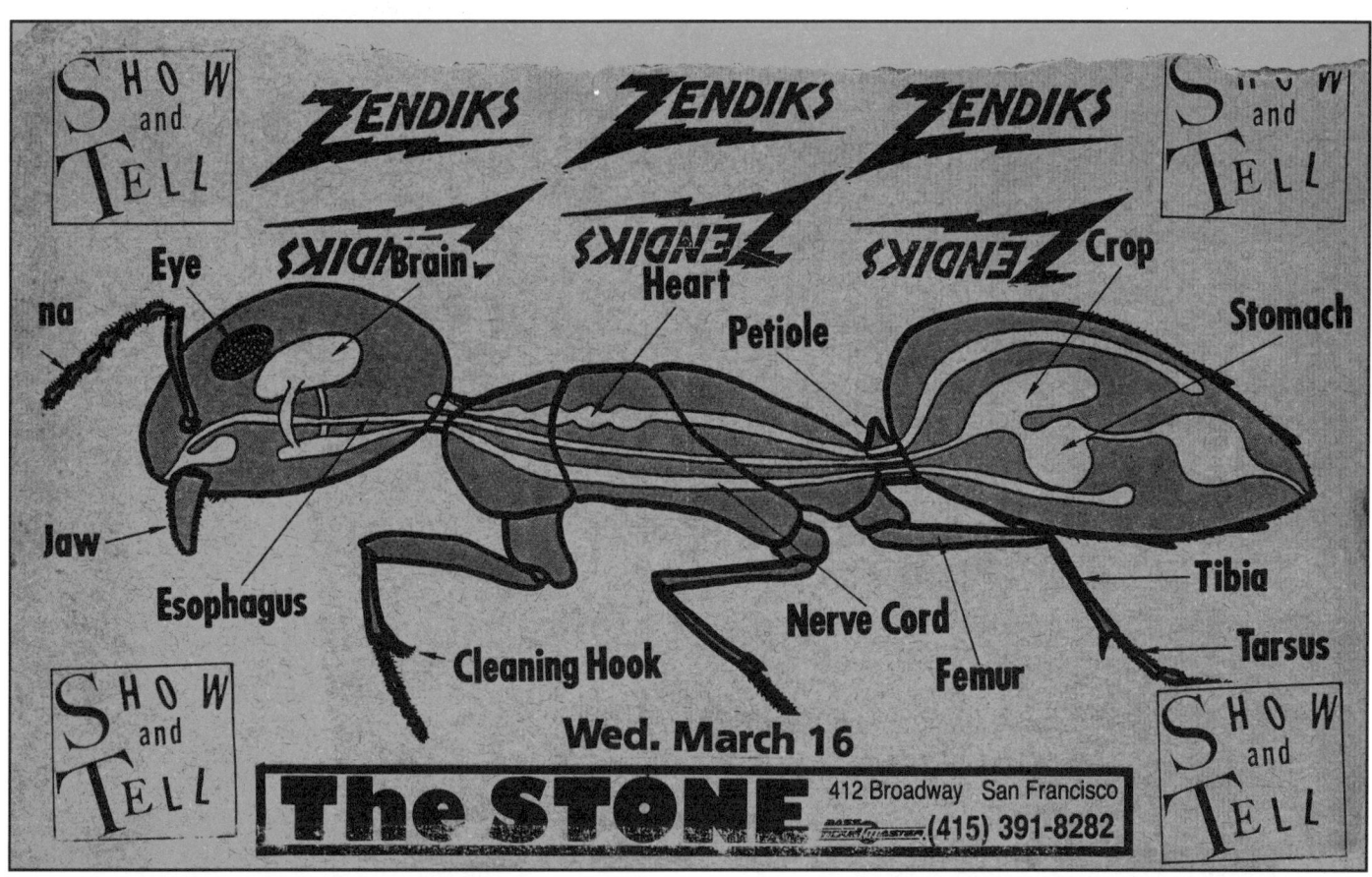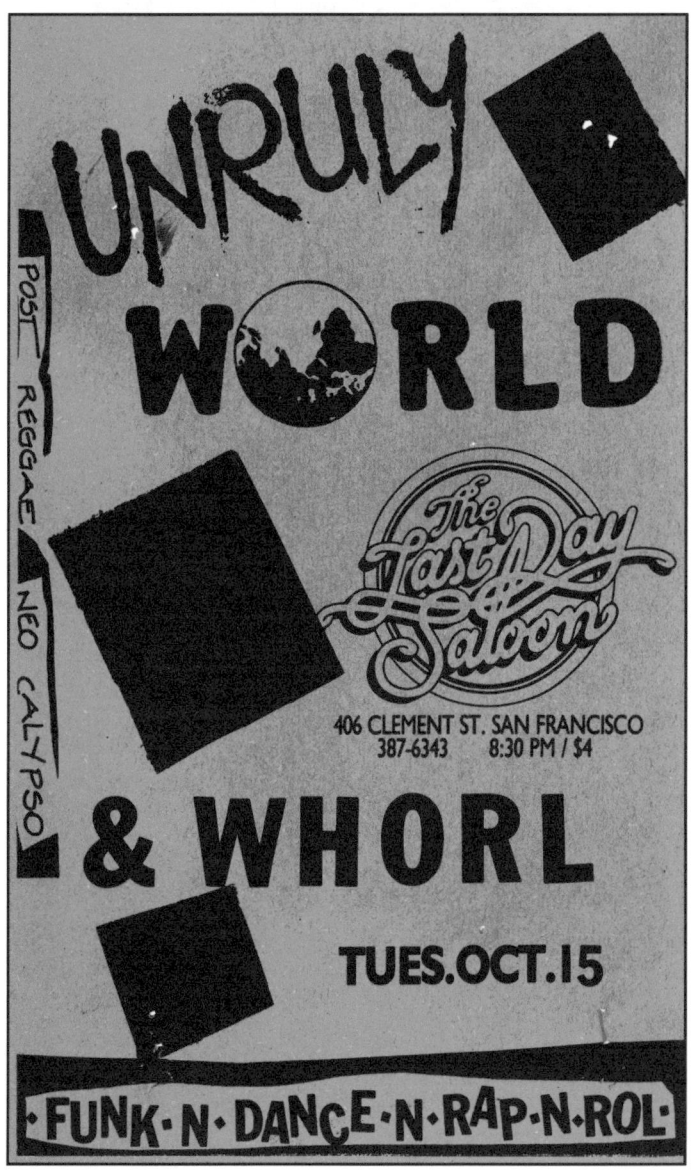

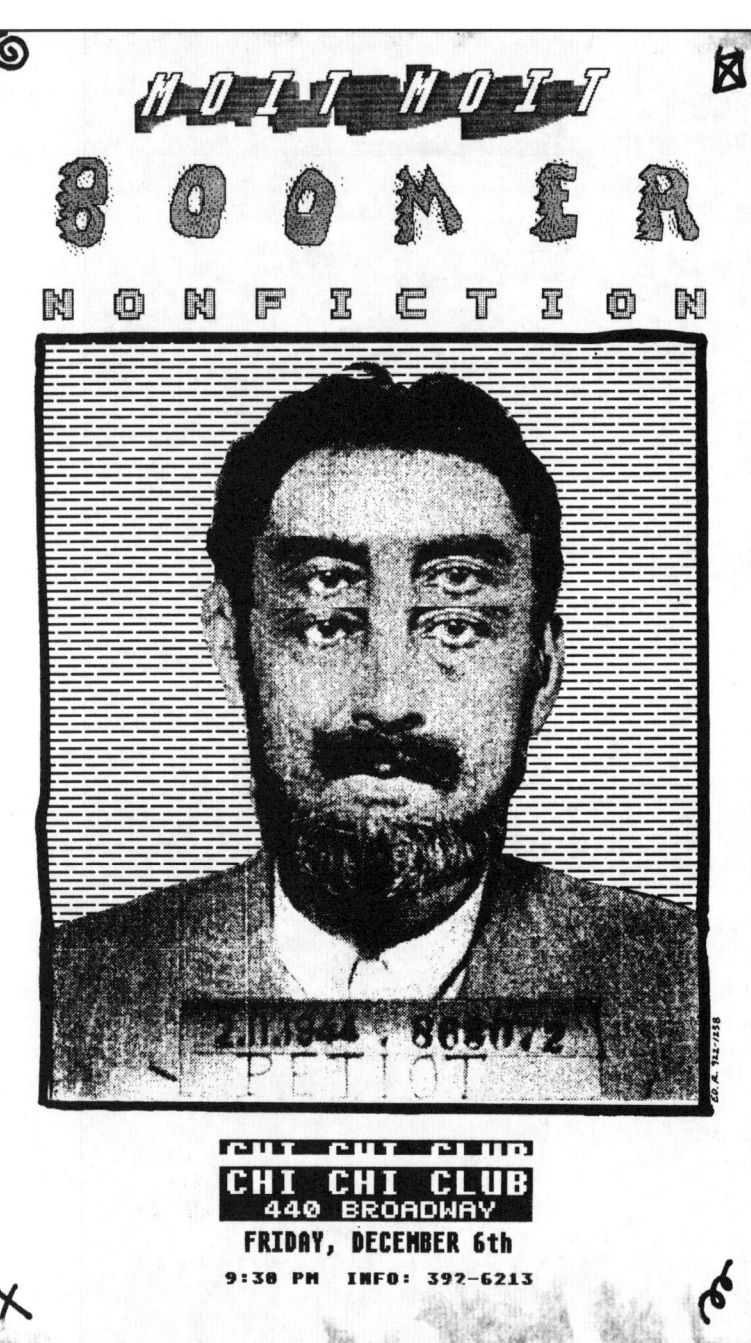

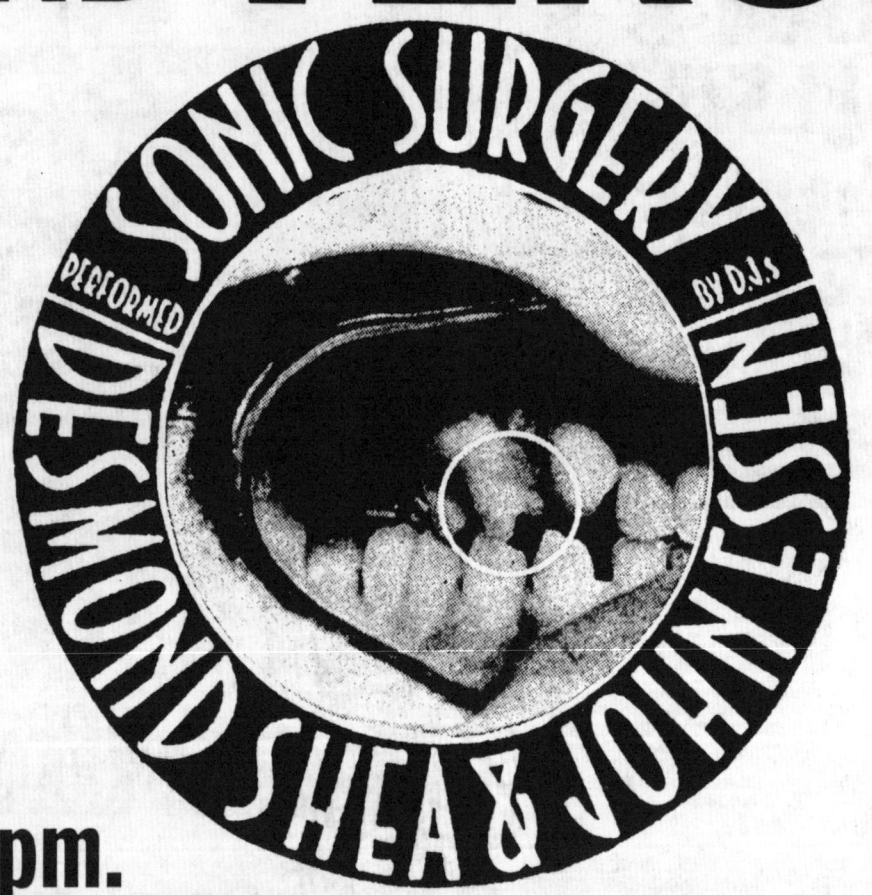

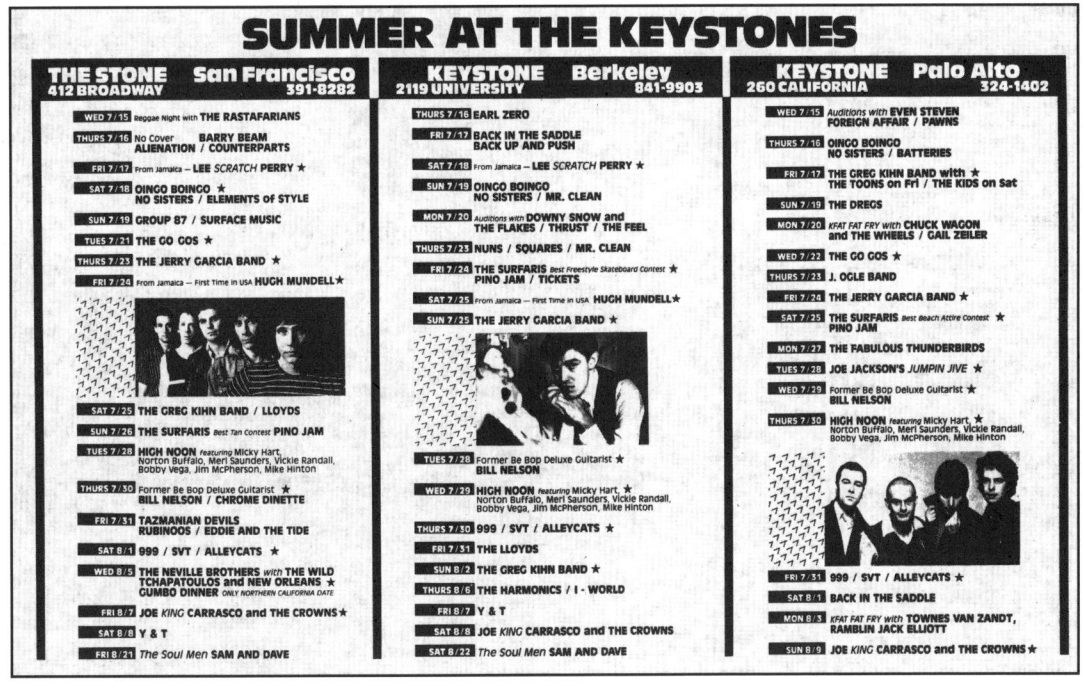

BENEFIT DANCE

PROCEEDS TO BENEFIT THE VICTIMS OF CHILE'S EARTHQUAKE

AN EVENING TO DANCE TO THE RHYTHM OF
"LATIN ALL STARS BAND"
SPECIAL PRESENTATION OF ARGENTINIAN TANGO
BY DEBORA MARTA

CHILEAN FOOD

SUNDAY, MAY 26 — 7 P.M.
CESAR'S PALACE
3140 MISSION ST. — SAN FRANCISCO

TICKETS: $5.00
AVAILABLE AT: DISCOTECA HABANA — DISCOLANDIA
LA GALLINITA MARKET — LIBRERIA MEXICO
AMERICAN MUSIC
FOR MORE INFORMATION CALL (415) 285-9564

GRAN BAILE A BENEFICIO
SPONSORED BY: CHILE COALITION

LAMBS BREAD

DANCE!

Thurs. DEC. 19
School's Out!

REGGAE

Ashkenaz
1317 San Pablo Ave.
Berk.

525-5054

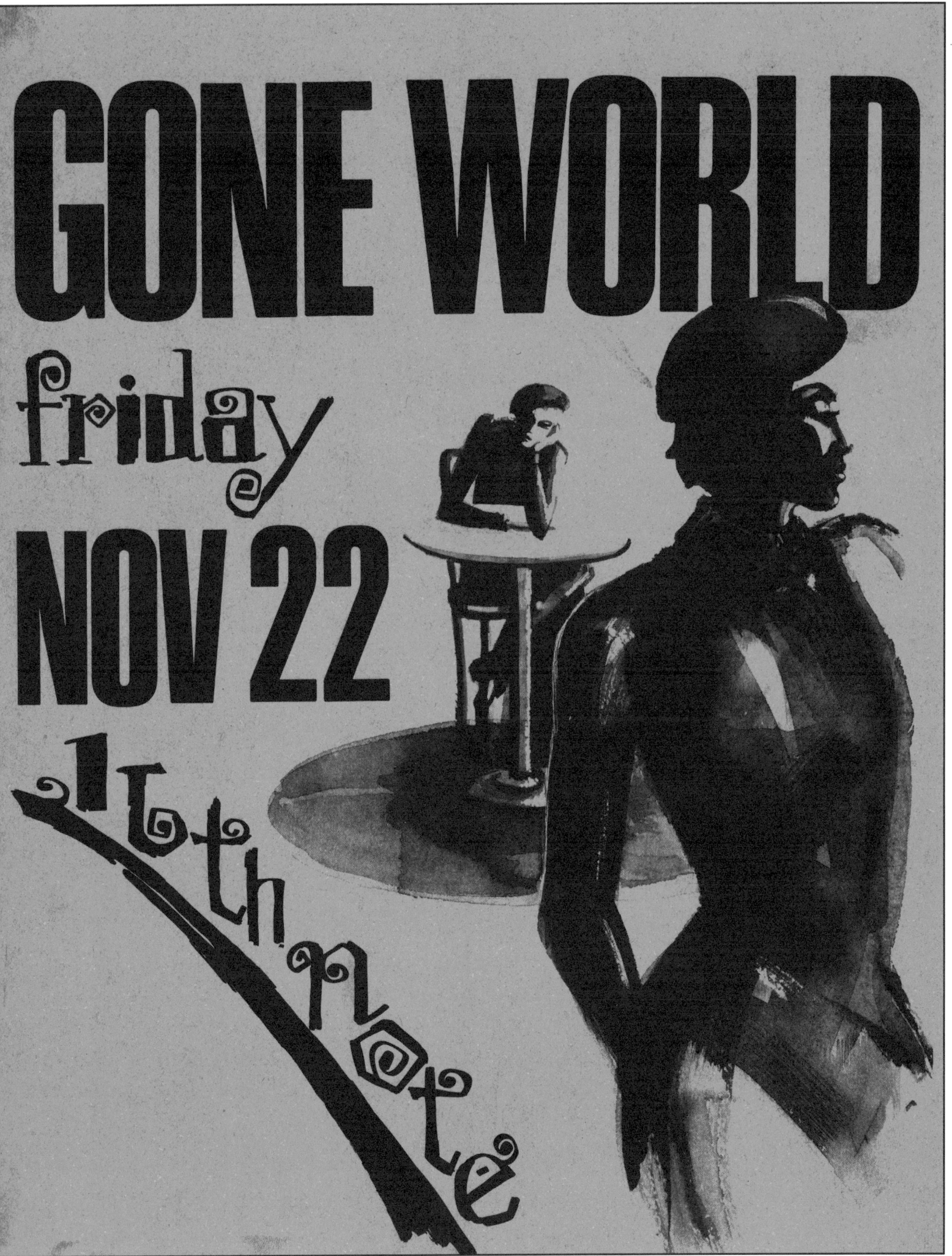

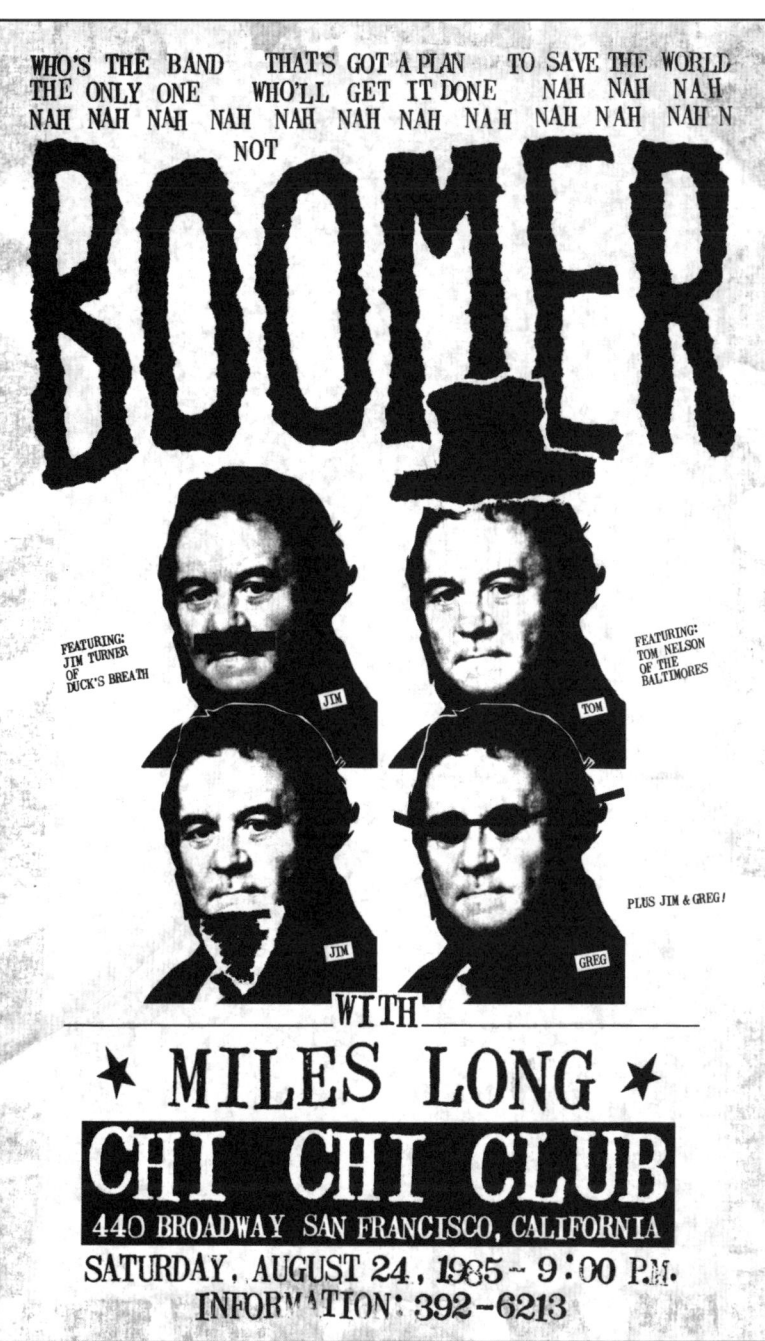

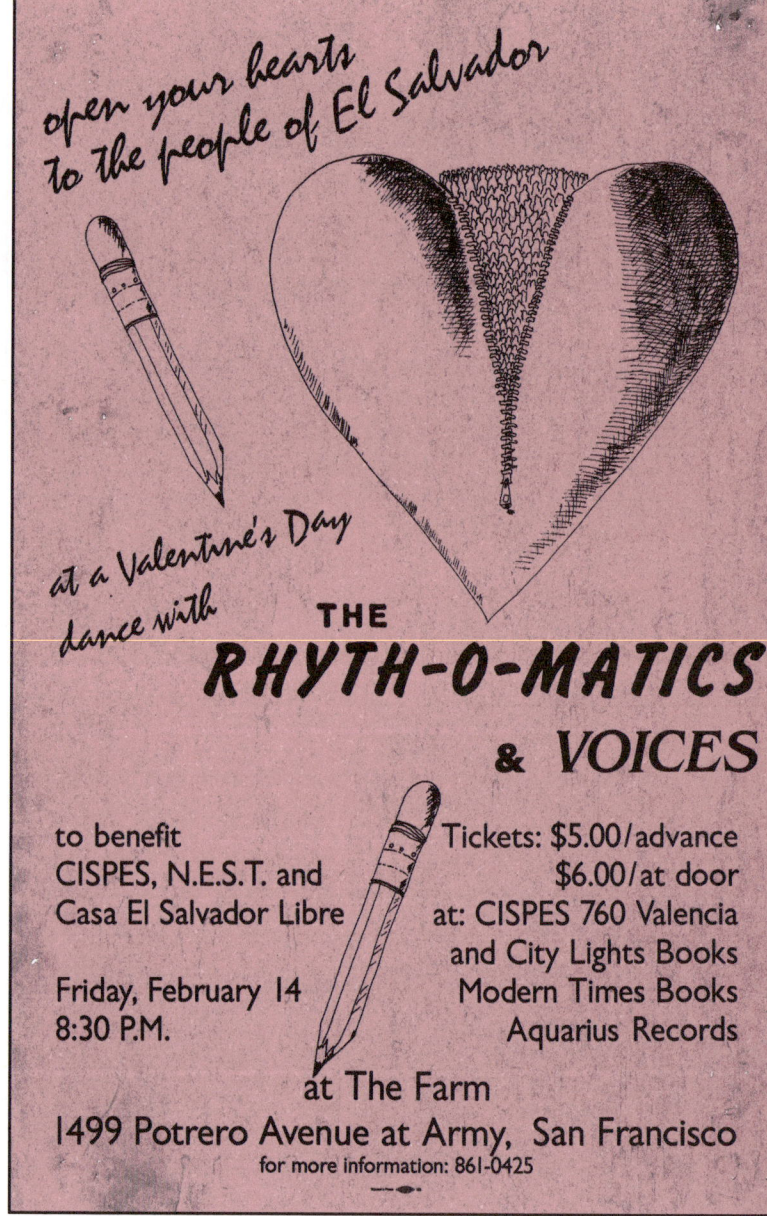

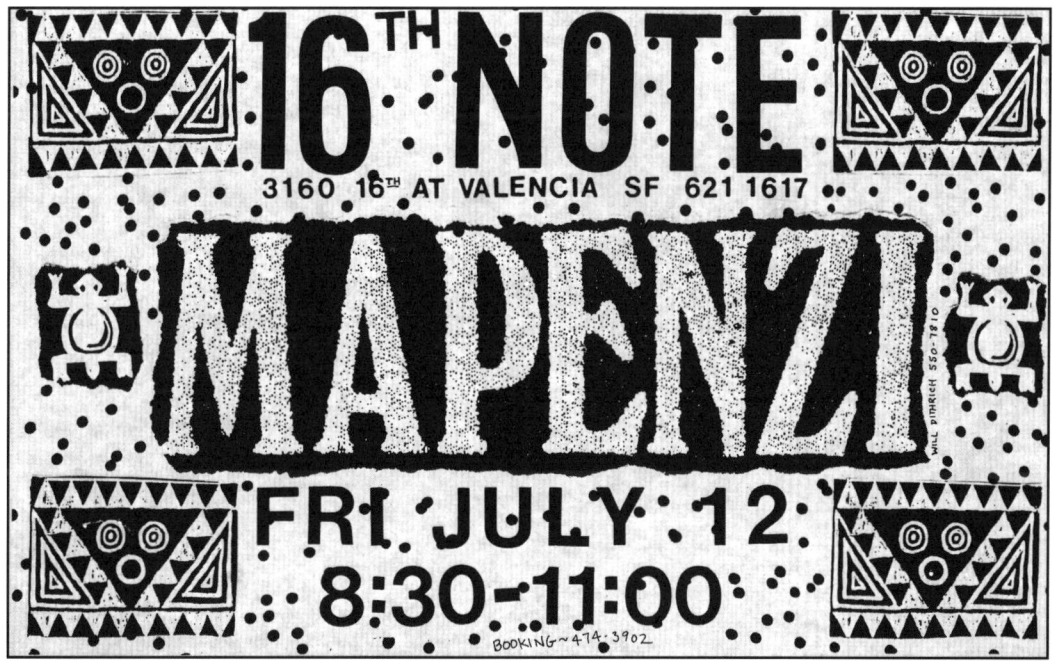

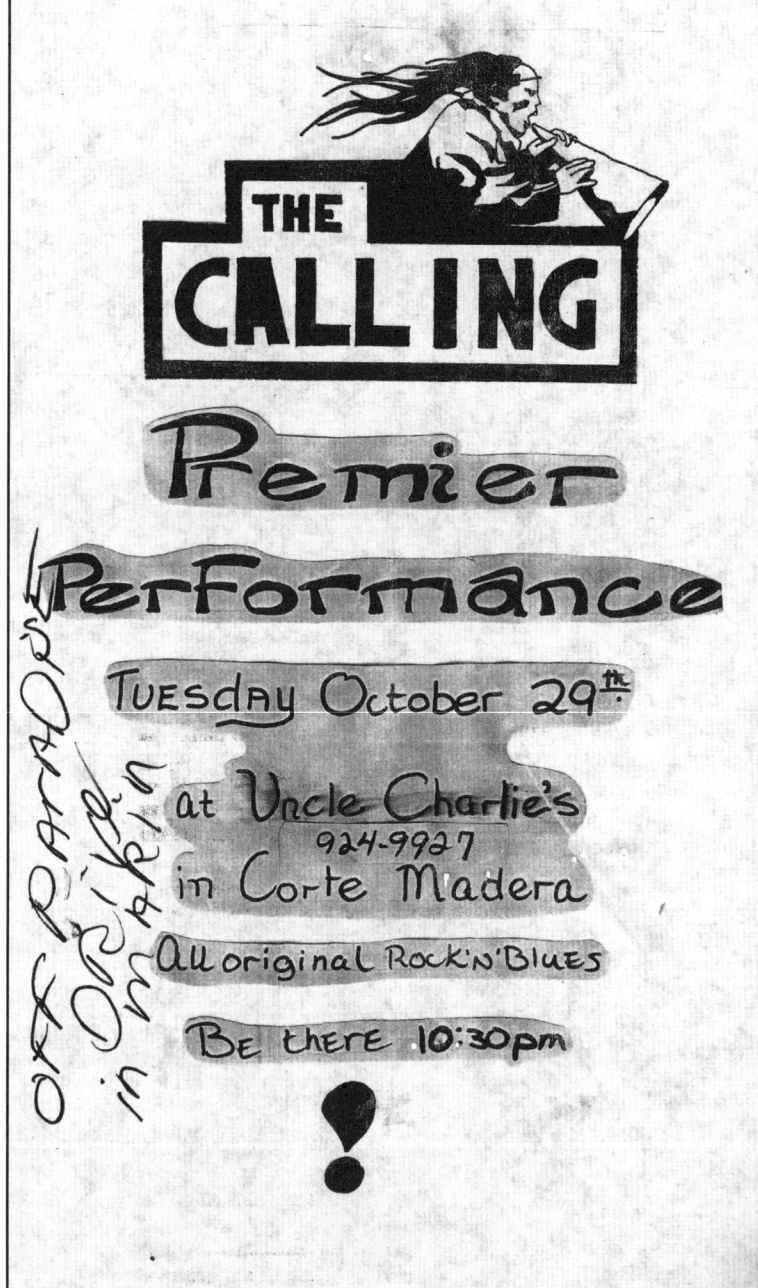

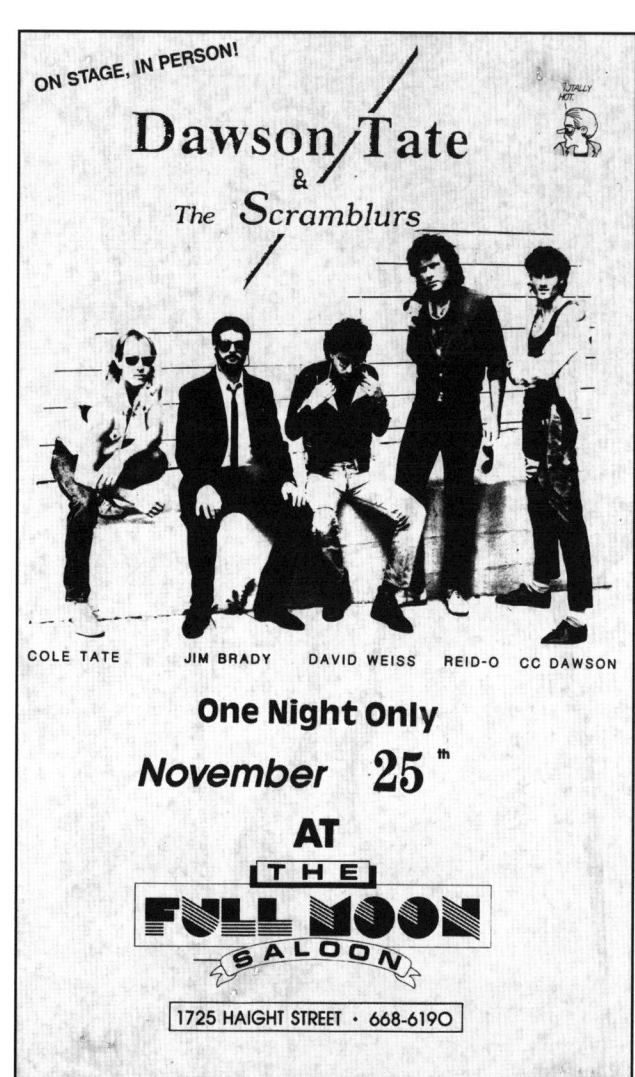

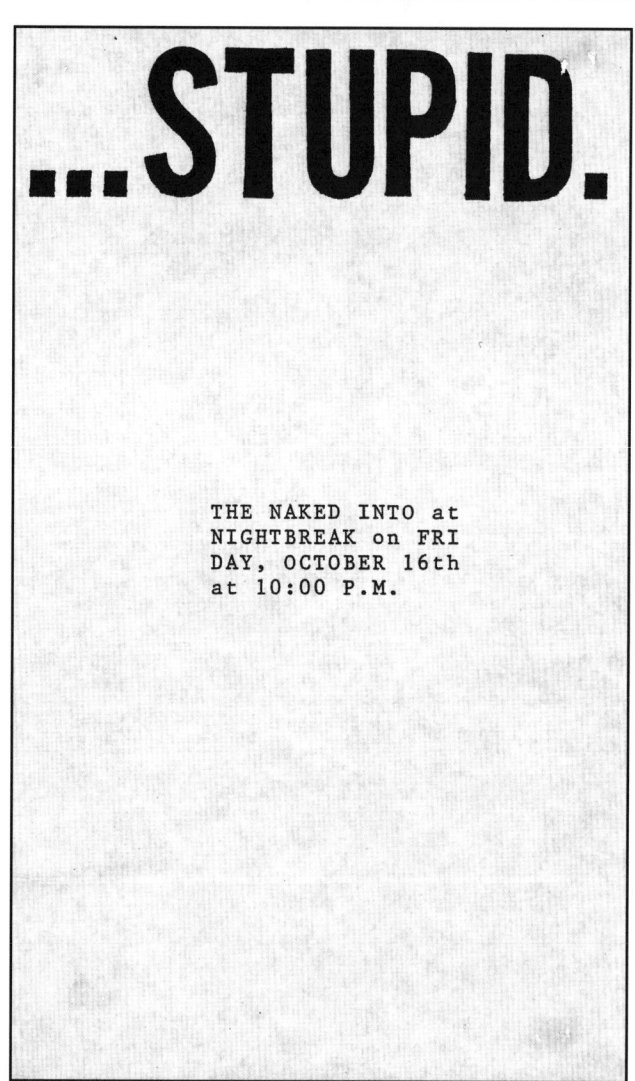

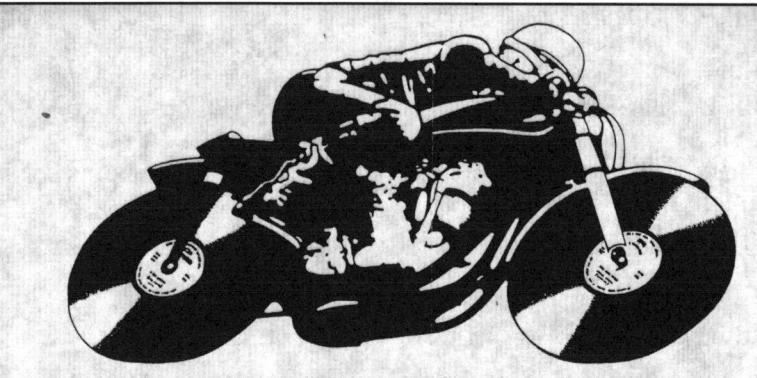

Speedway Records

5:00pm MON. FEB. 29th IN-STORE WITH

the leather nun

FEATURING BIKER MOVIES
'HELL'S ANGELS '69' / 'HELL'S ANGELS ON WHEELS'

AT NIGHTBREAK/SPEEDWAY RECORDS
1821 HAIGHT ST.

THE LEATHER NUN....LIVE at THE I-BEAM....MONDAY FEB. 29....DOORS 9pm

ESKIMO
AND THE SQUARE ROOTS

TUES MAR 8
MUSICWORKS
ON MARKET AT CHURCH, S.F.

LAST CHANCE TO SEE ESKIMO BEFORE THEIR NORTHWEST TOUR!

WITH: THE RESPONSIBLES
AND
GUNGA DIN

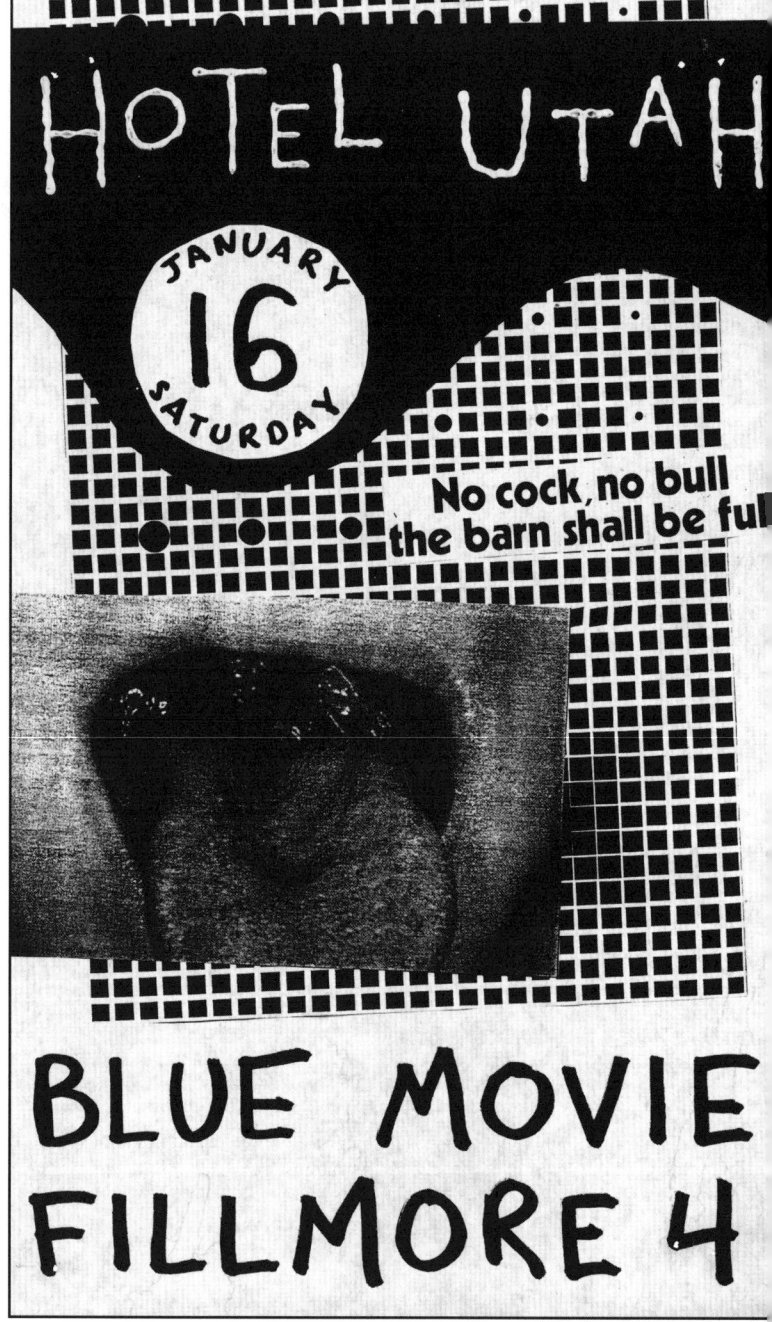

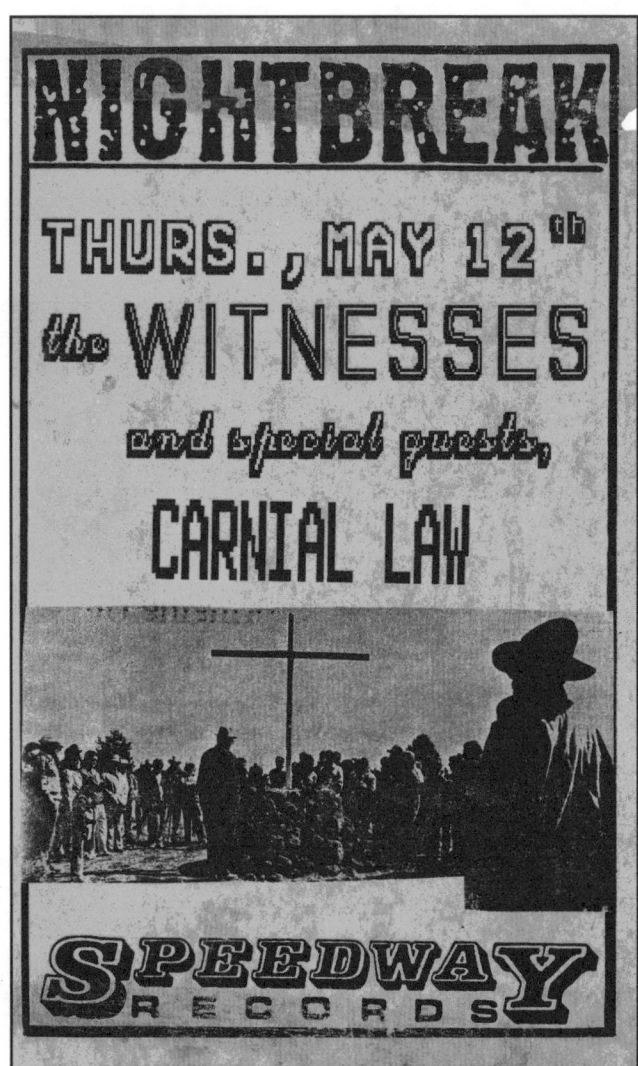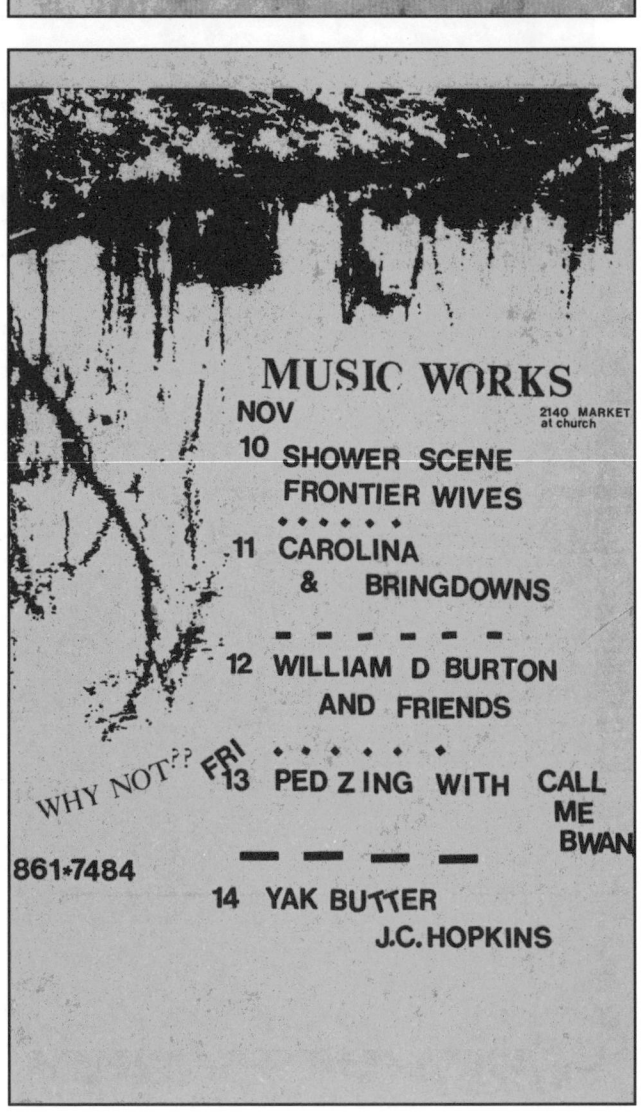

BAM & KUSF PRESENT

MONKEY RHYTHM

SHY HANDS

INNER CITY

THURSDAY, NOVEMBER 7, 8 P.M.

THE STONE, S.F., 412 BROADWAY

ALL AGES WELCOME

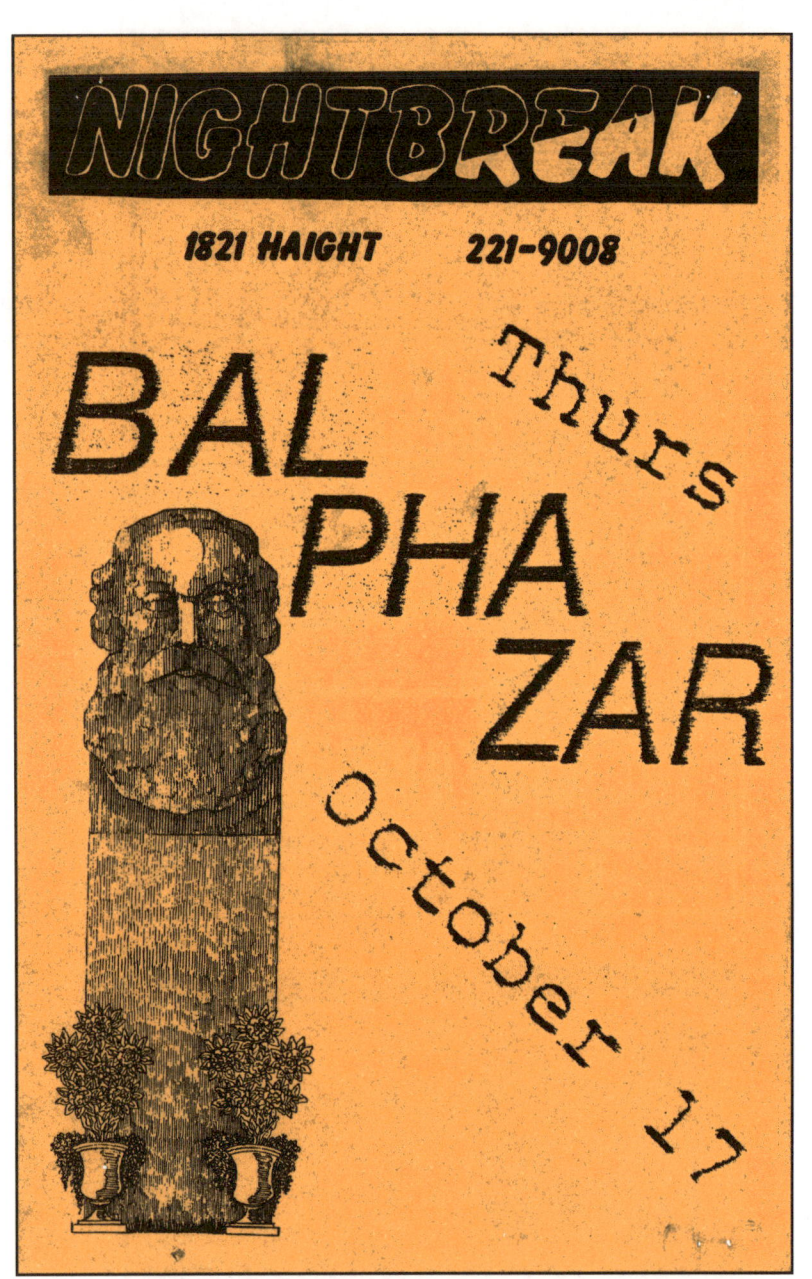

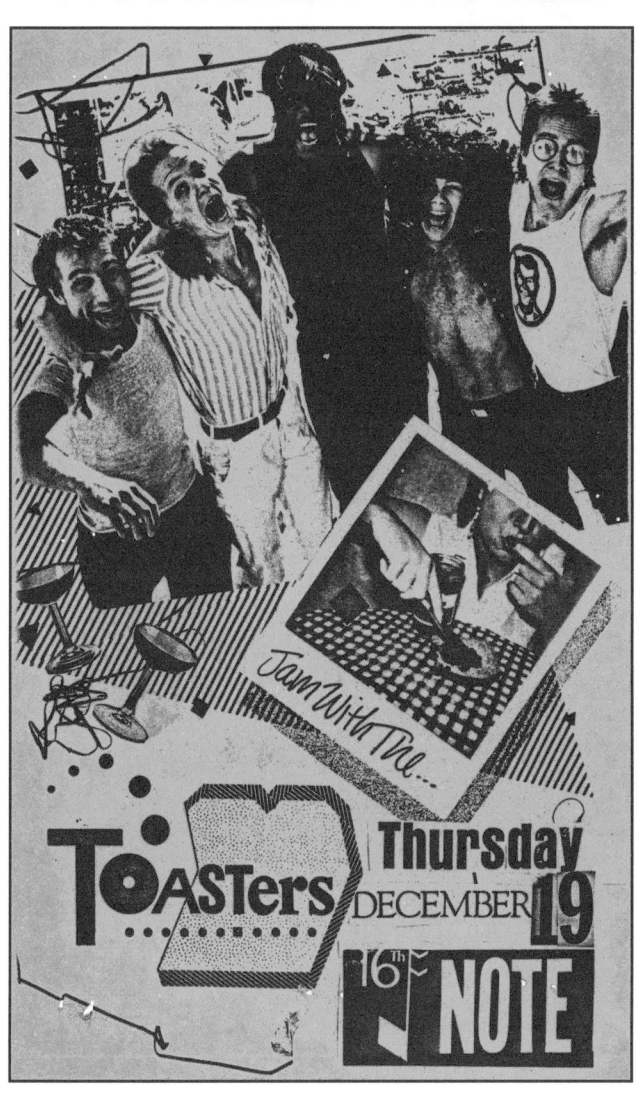

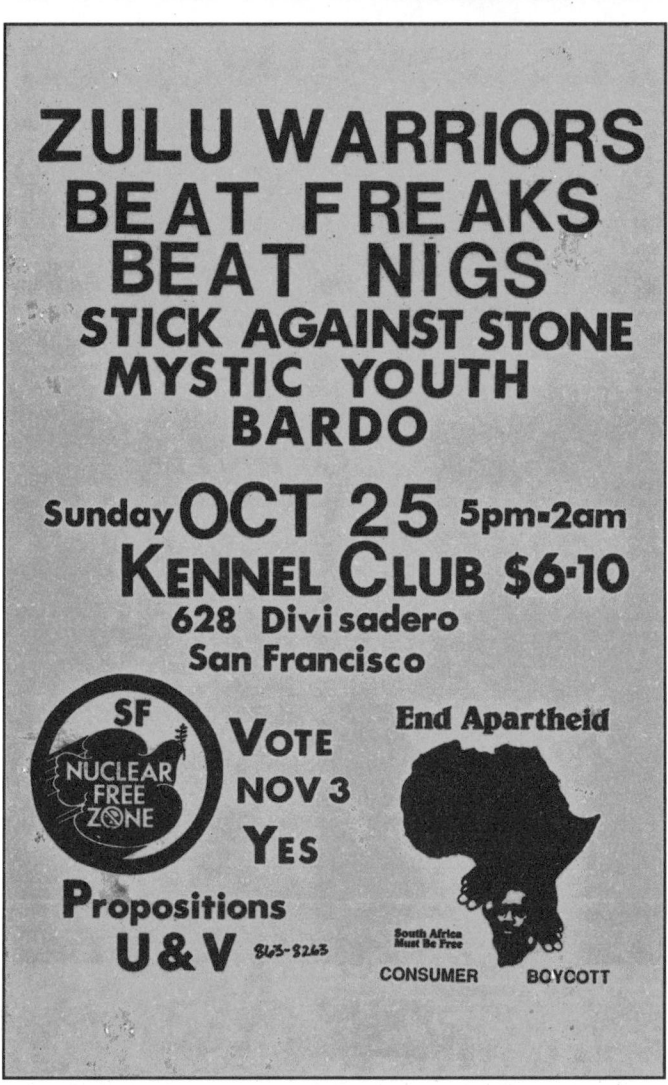

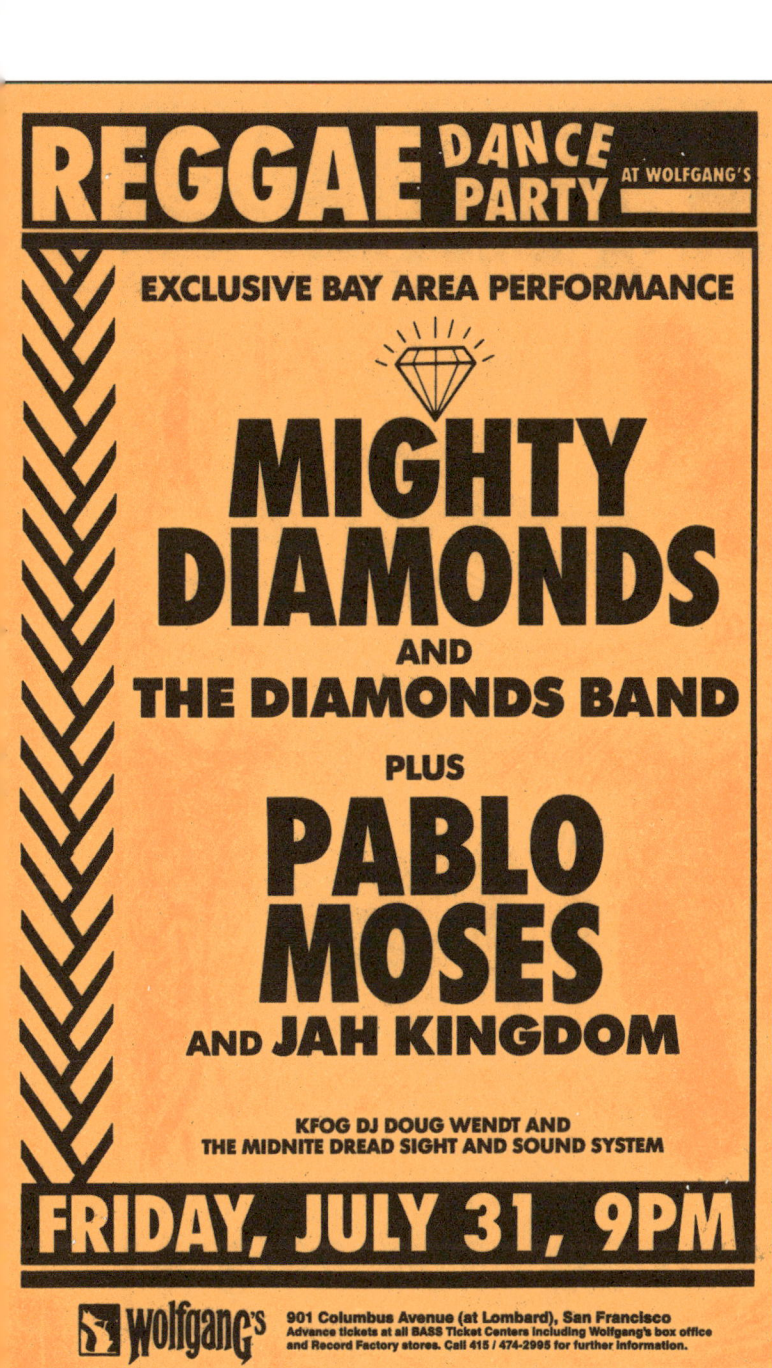

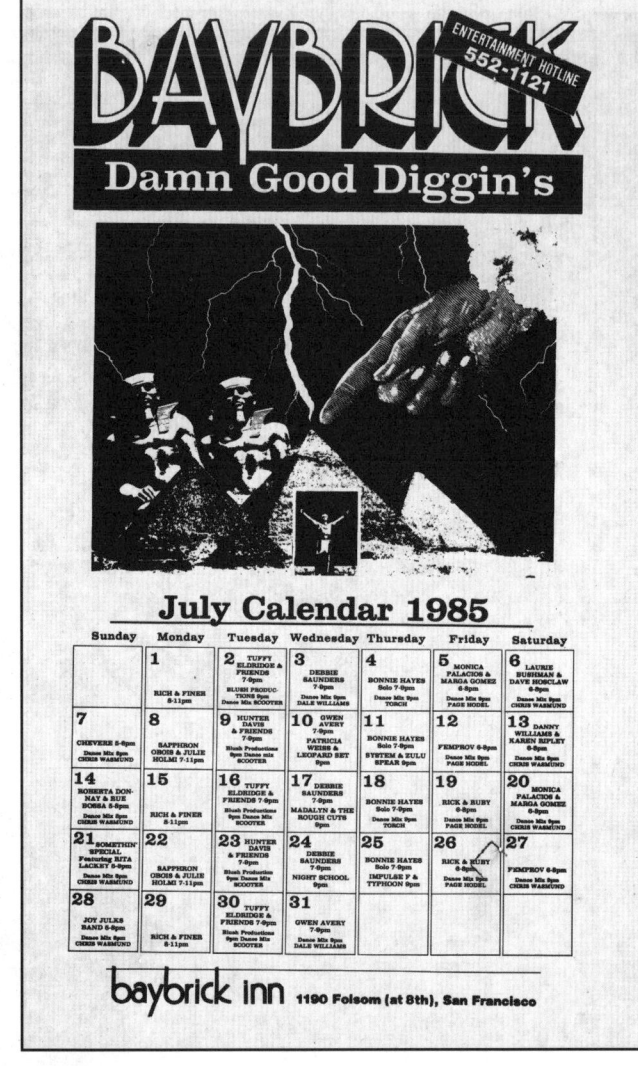

COME to the unveiling of the front door of

IZZIE GOMEZ'

Renowned speakeasy and saloon of the '30s and '40s. At the Vesuvio Cafe, 255 Columbus Ave. on Thursday February 19 at 6 p.m. Many celebrities will be present including Joe the Goop, Black Hand Pete, Shortie "The Ace" Pistola and Charlie "Give me a Hot Dog" Minchiarelli. Master of ceremonies and guest of honor: Neil Hitt, San Francisco Chronicle.

CELEBRATE! THE RESURRECTION

A 12 HOUR ORGY OF NON-STOP MUSIC AND LIGHTS

TO BENEFIT JERRY ABRAMS HEAD LIGHTS

STARRING

BARRY MELTON-SPENCER DRYDEN & FRIENDS

THE SUNDAE KNIGHT BANNED

GREEN ONIONS   IMPERIALIST

THE MUVIES

BOOTS   THE SYNC

VISUAL STIMULATION BY
JERRY ABRAMS HEAD LIGHTS

SUNDAY, AUGUST 25th, 1985

at the

STARRY PLOUGH
3101 Shattuck Ave., Berkeley
DOORS OPEN AT 2 pm—FIRST SET 2:30pm
Psychedelic Pspaghetti —Lunch & Dinner
Admission $5.00 at the door

From South Africa

THE MALOPOETS

Thursday August 29th
THE STONE 412 Broadway
S.F. 391-8282
The True Pulse of the World Beat
Advance tickets available through BASS
with ROGIE'S MUYEI AFRICA
DJ Jonathon E.

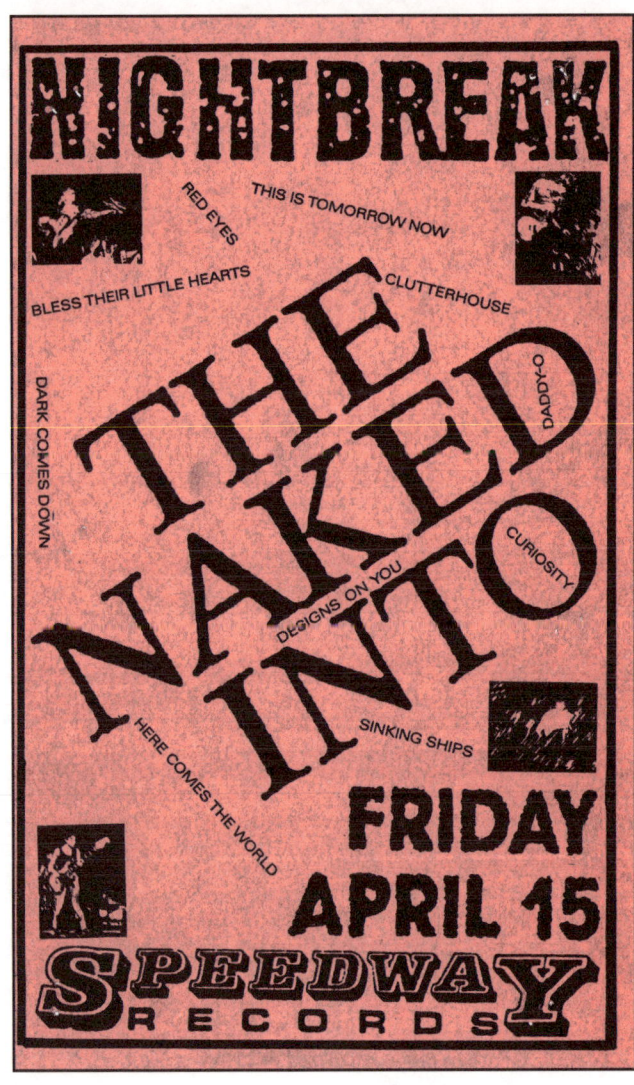

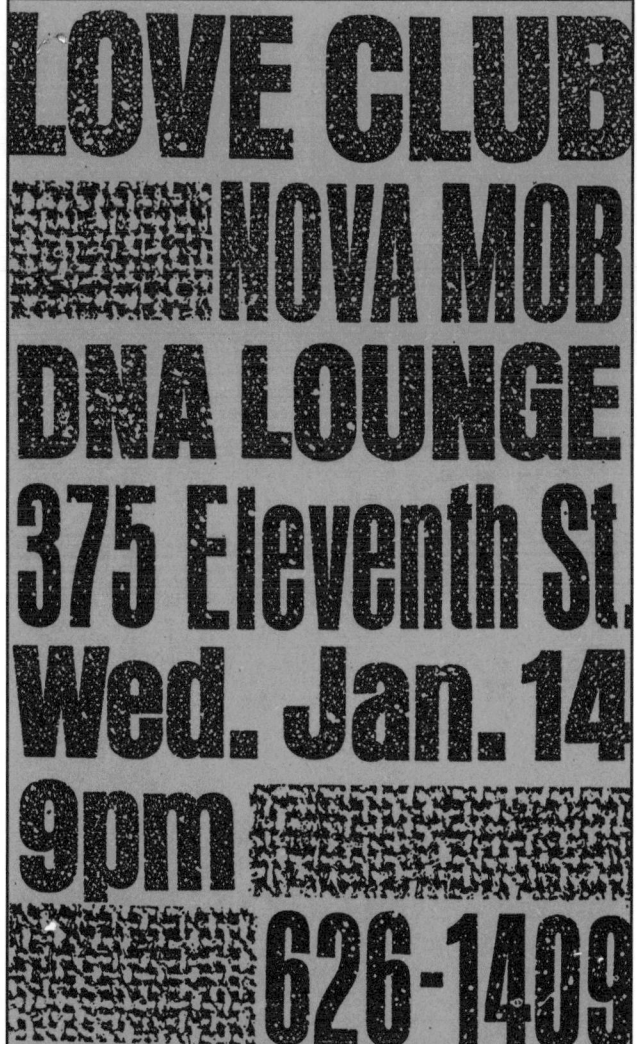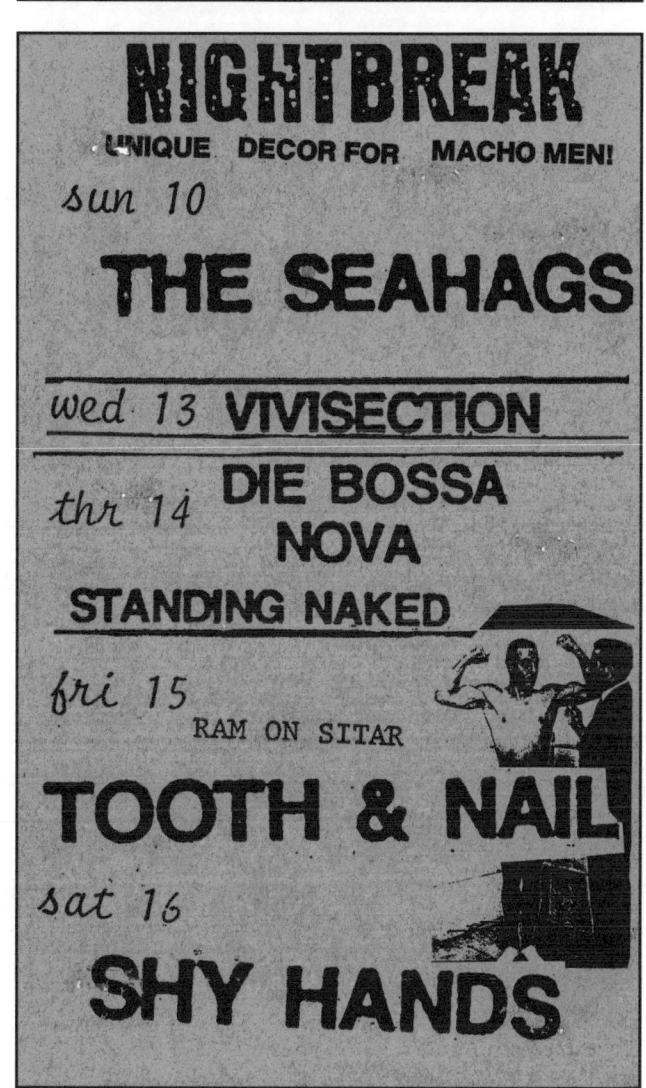

OLUFUMNI PRESENTS

REGGAE RAP PARTY

MEDITATIONS reggae band

RYTH-O-MATICS "WORLD BEAT"

 HIP HOP

JULY 6

9 PM

$10

RUSSIAN HALL 2460 SUTTER ST. SF

FRIDAY MAY 24

STICK FIGURES

FULL MOON SALOON

1725 HAIGHT

9:30

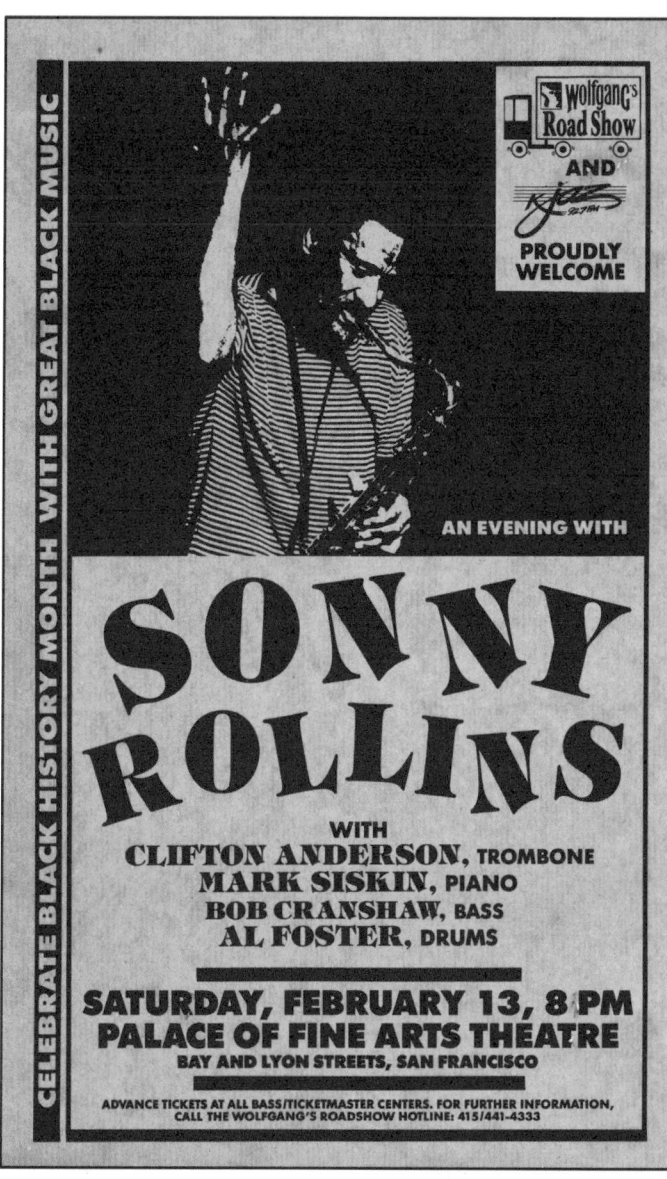

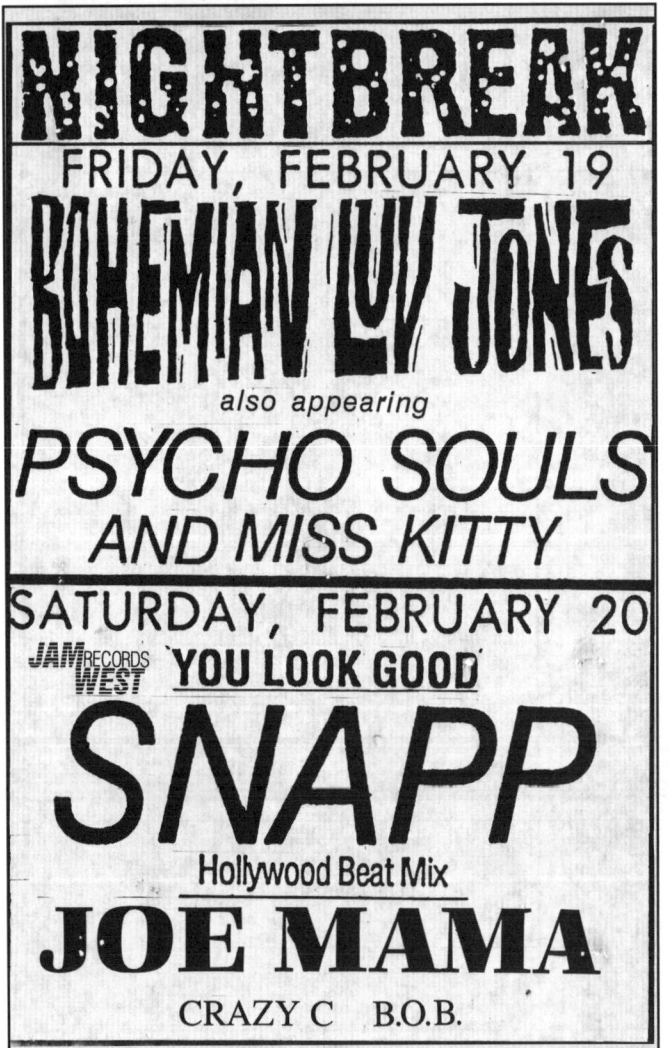

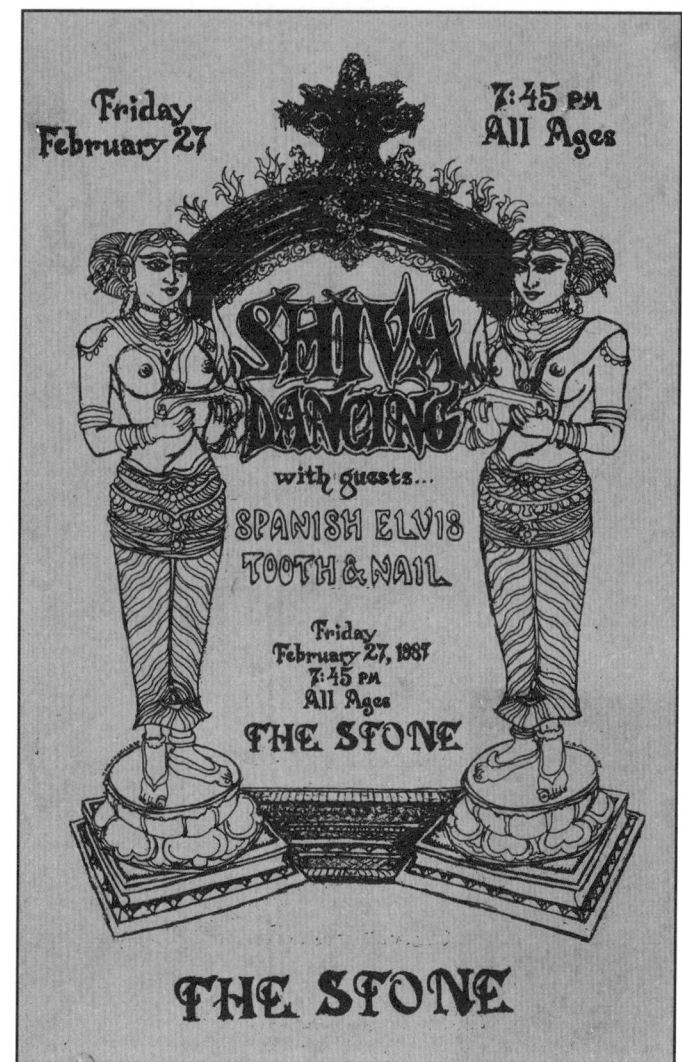

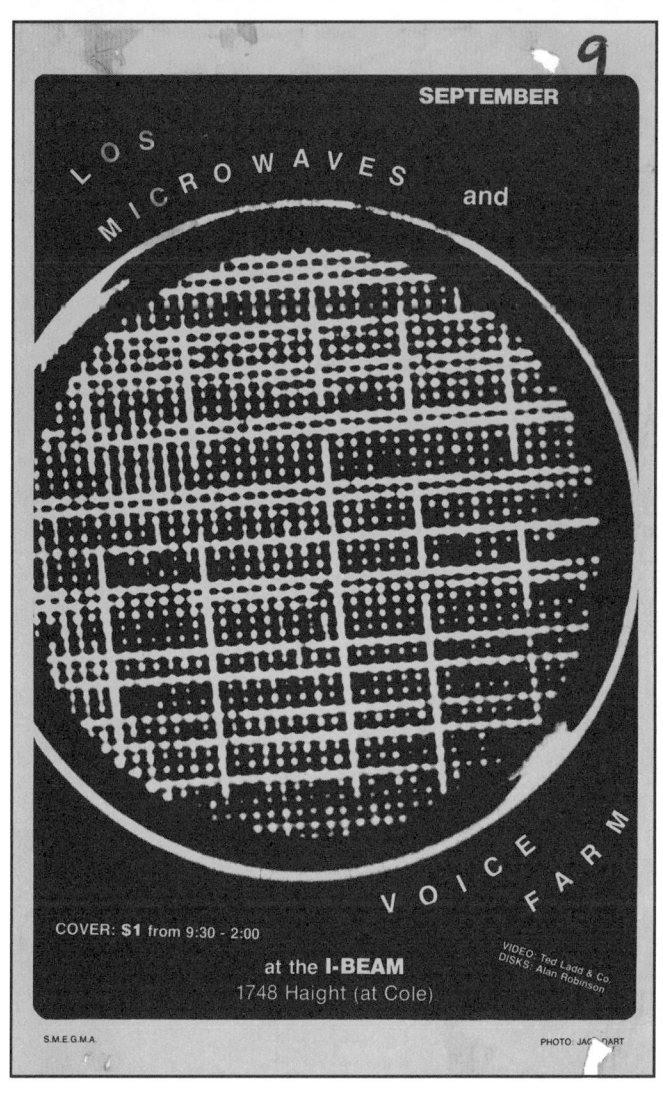

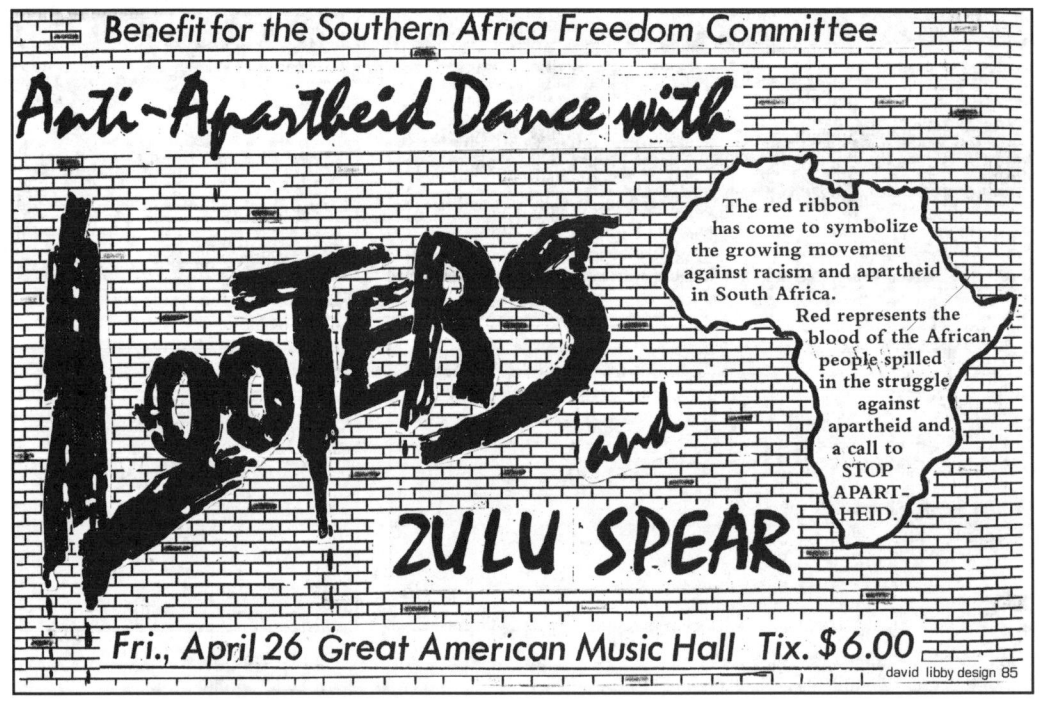

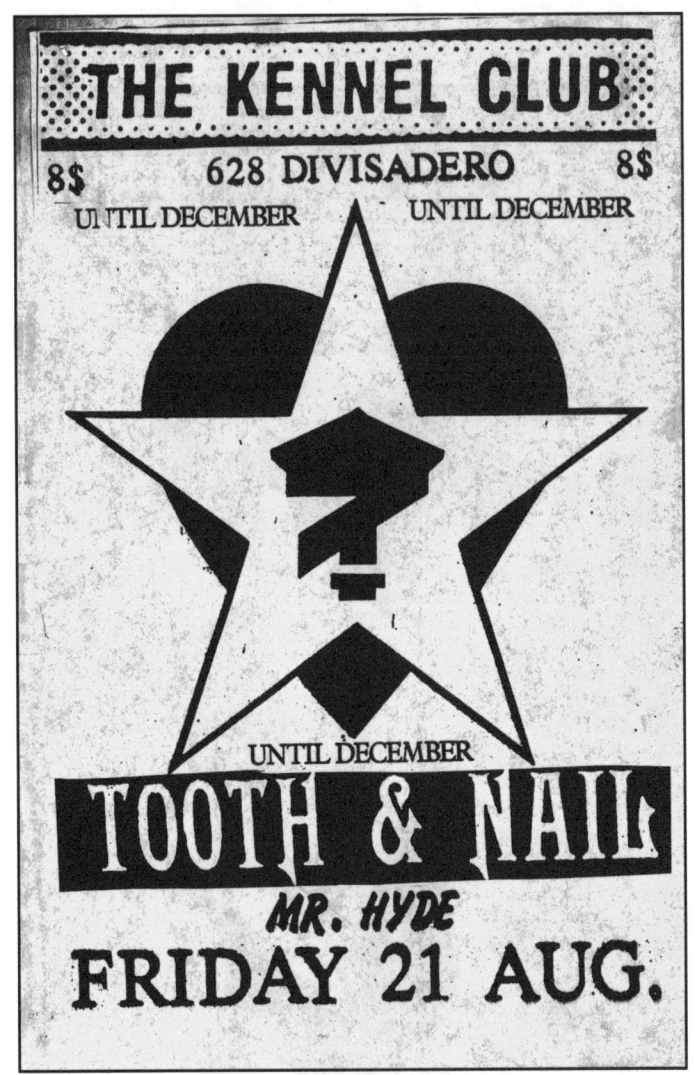

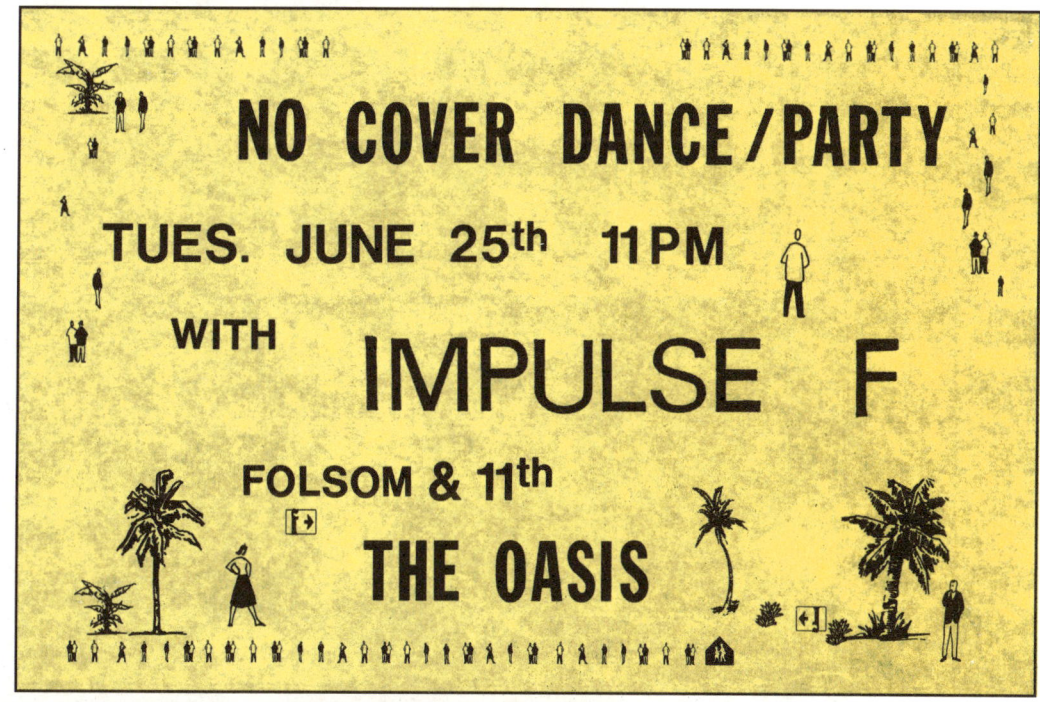

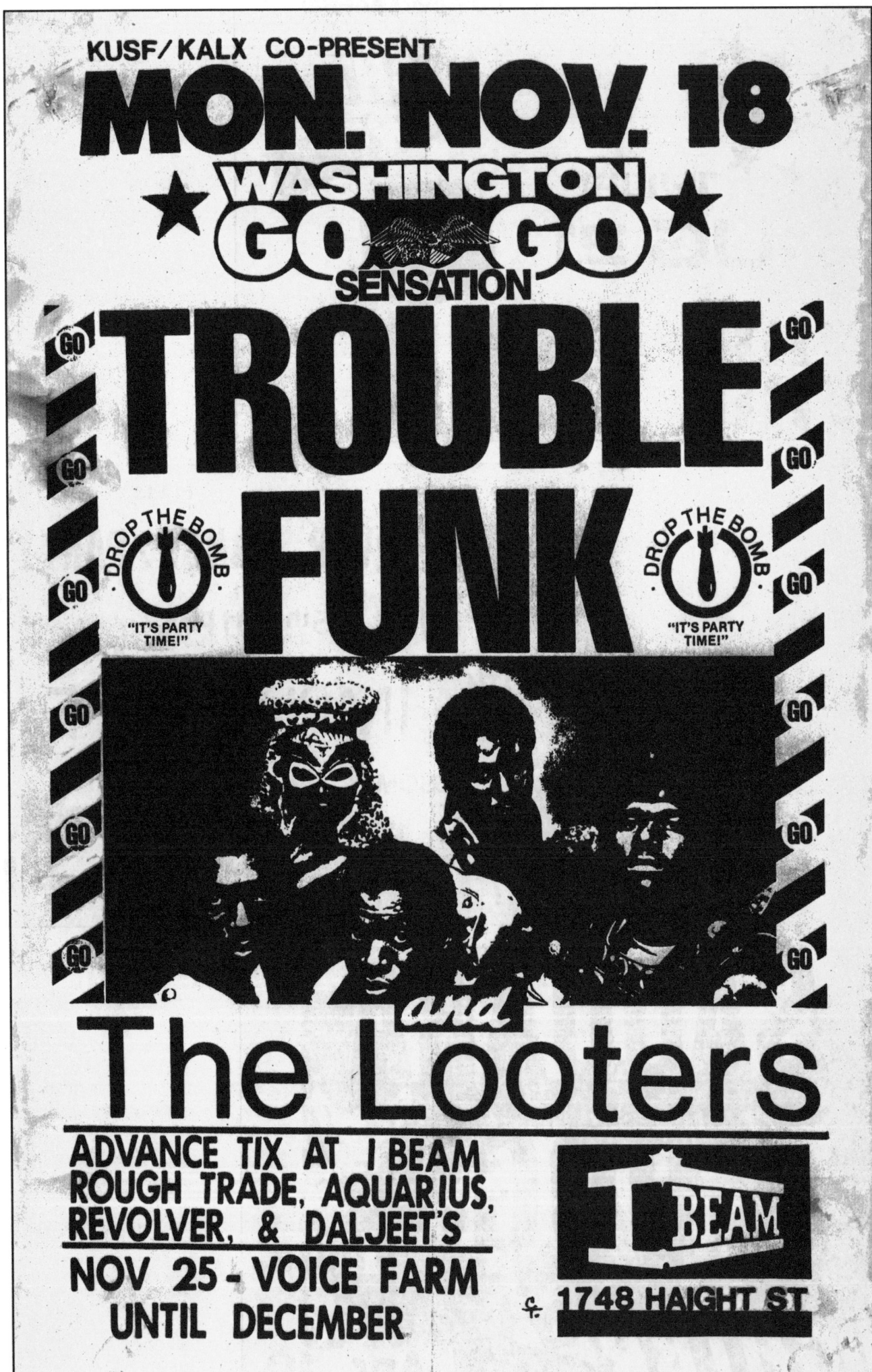

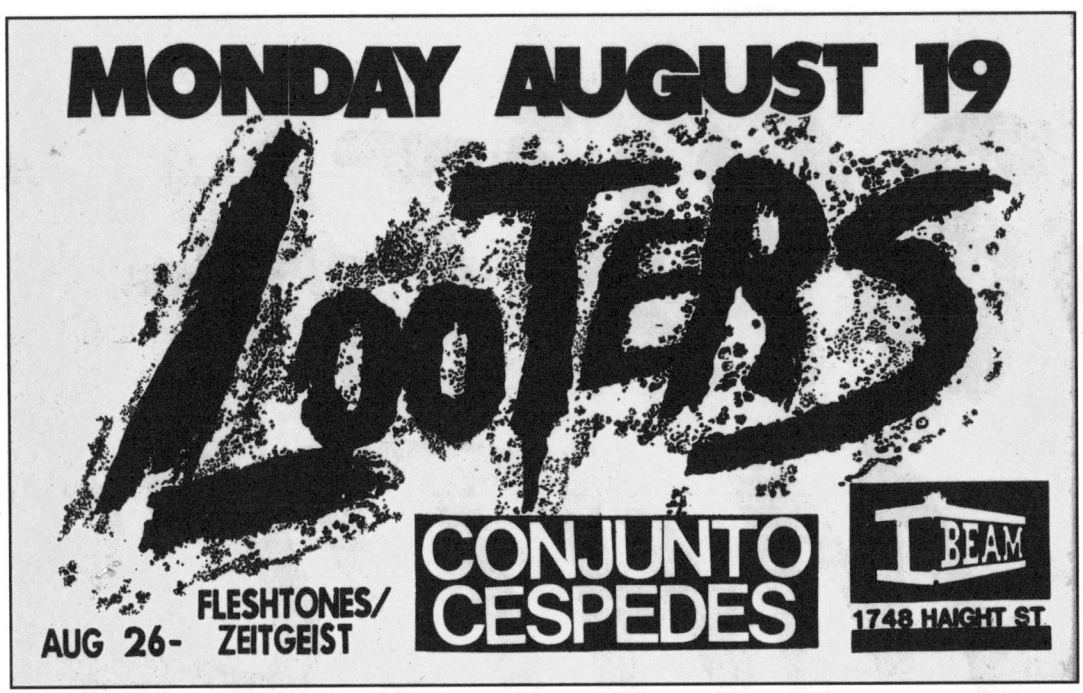

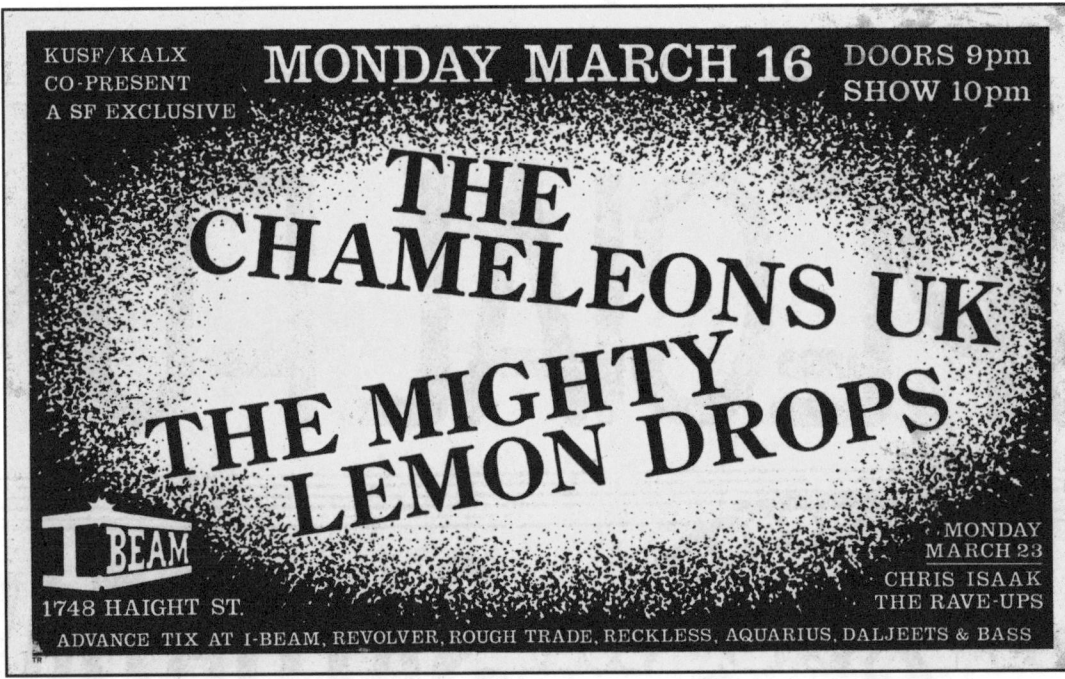

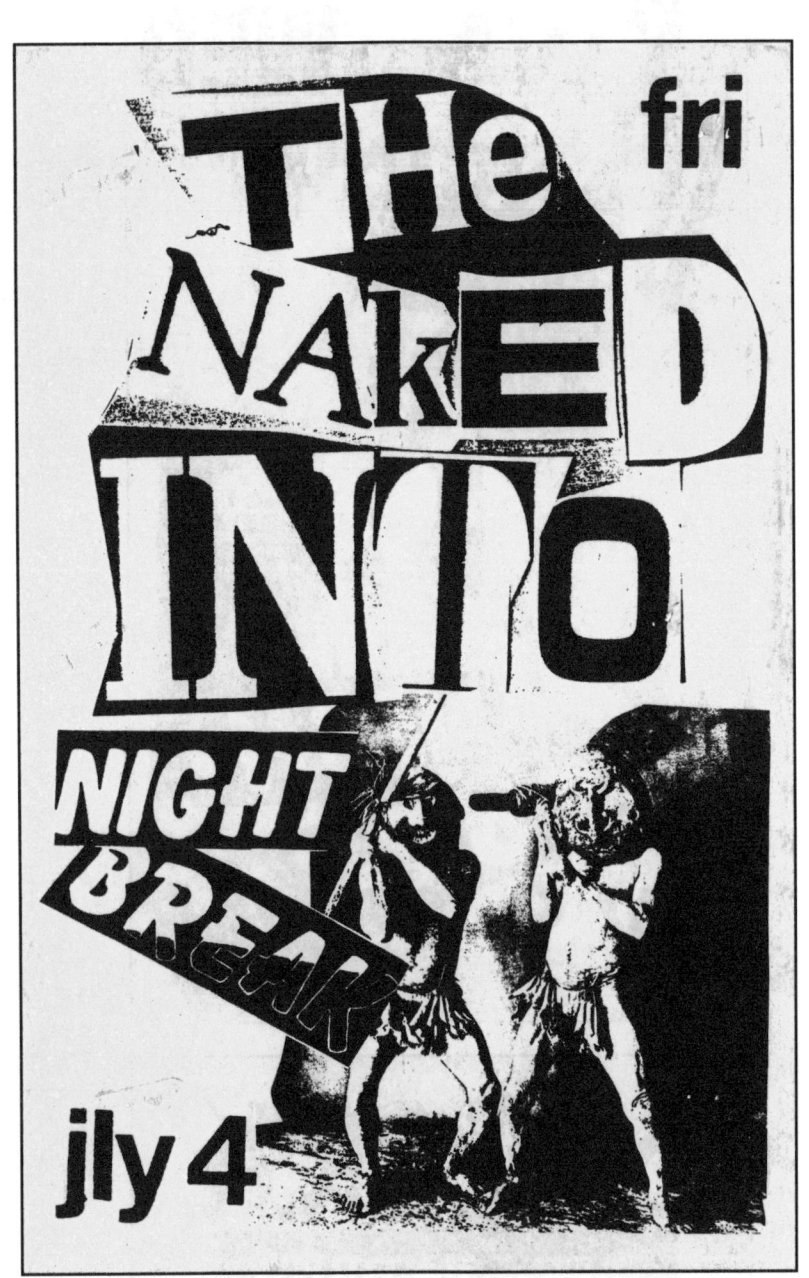

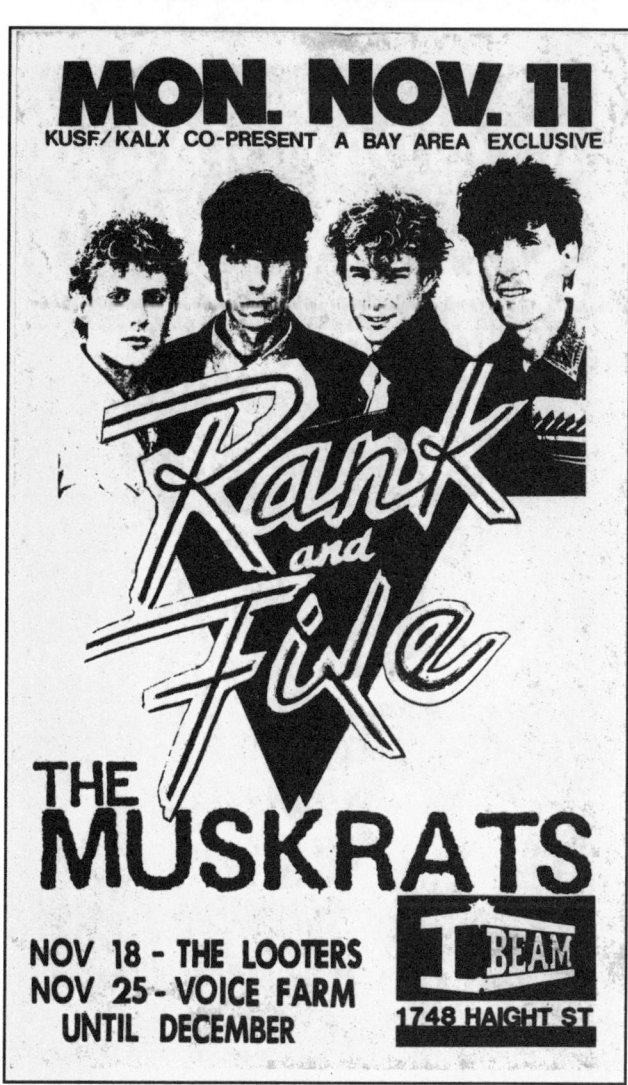
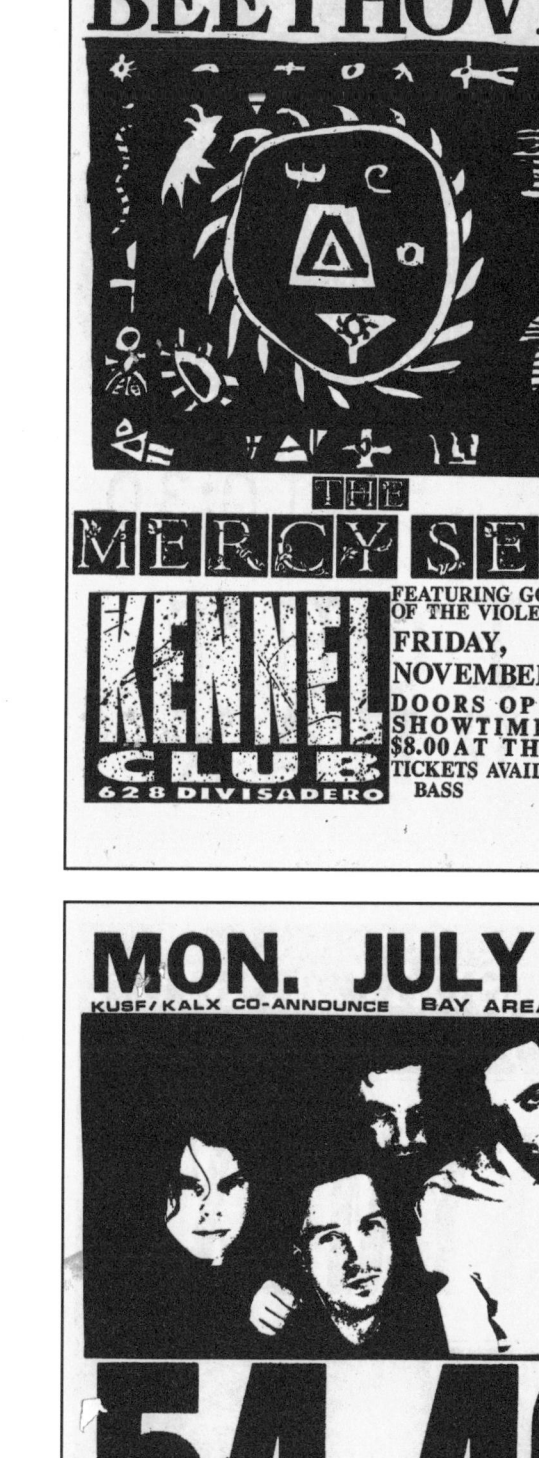

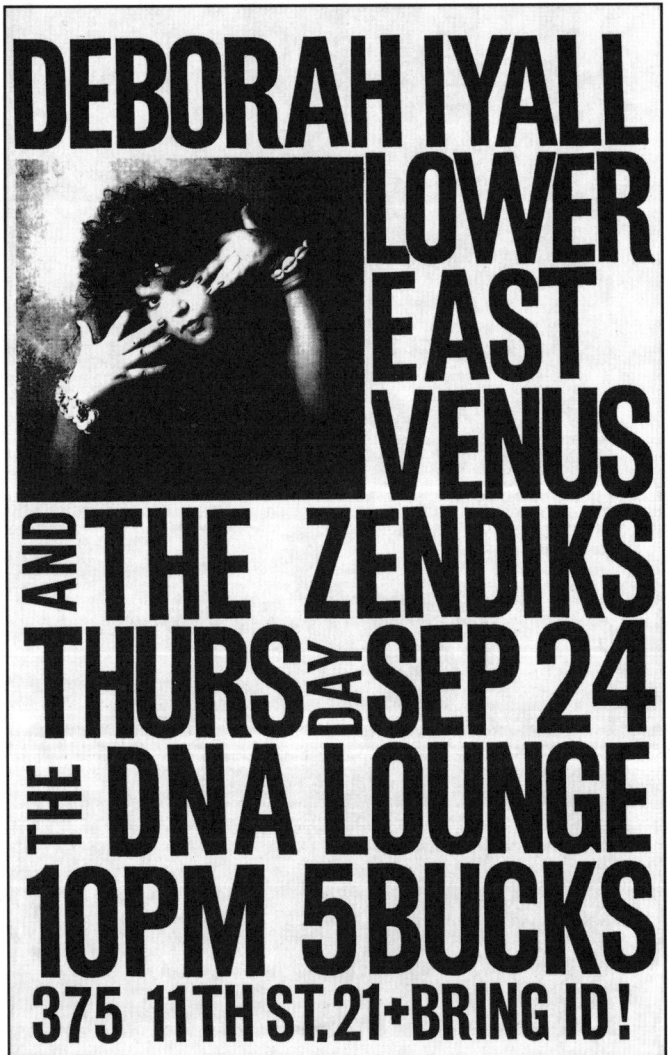

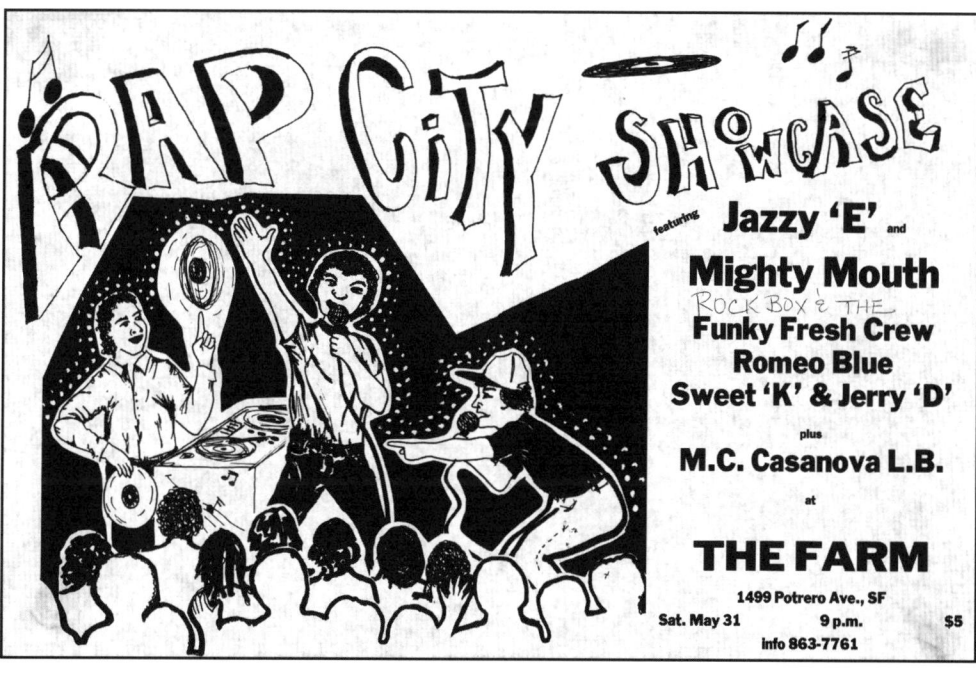

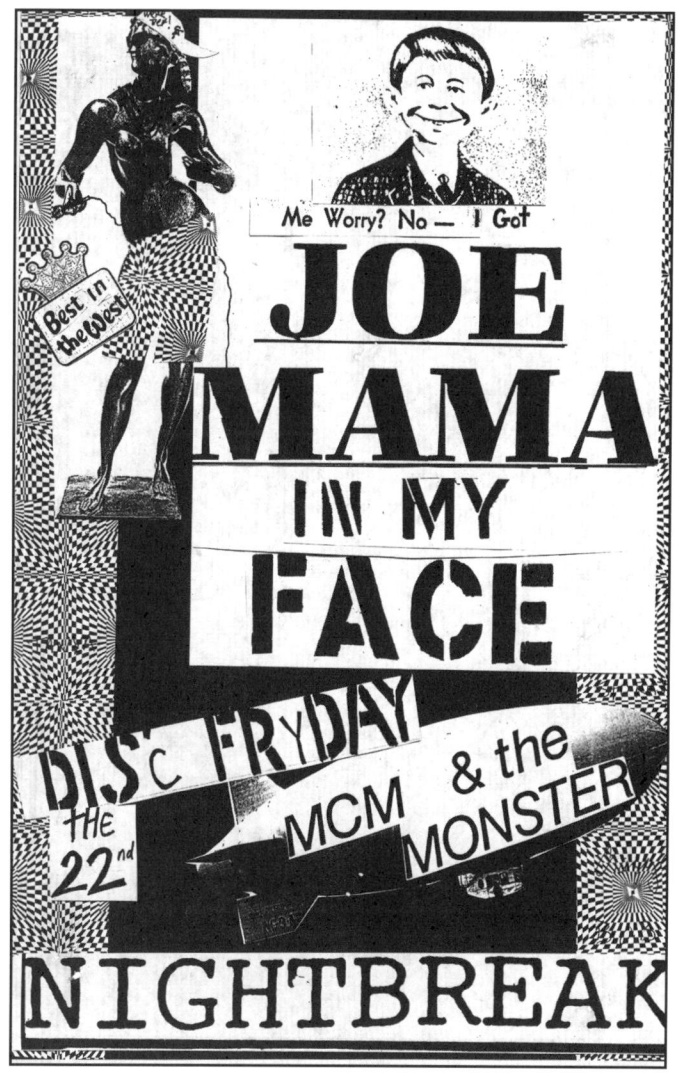

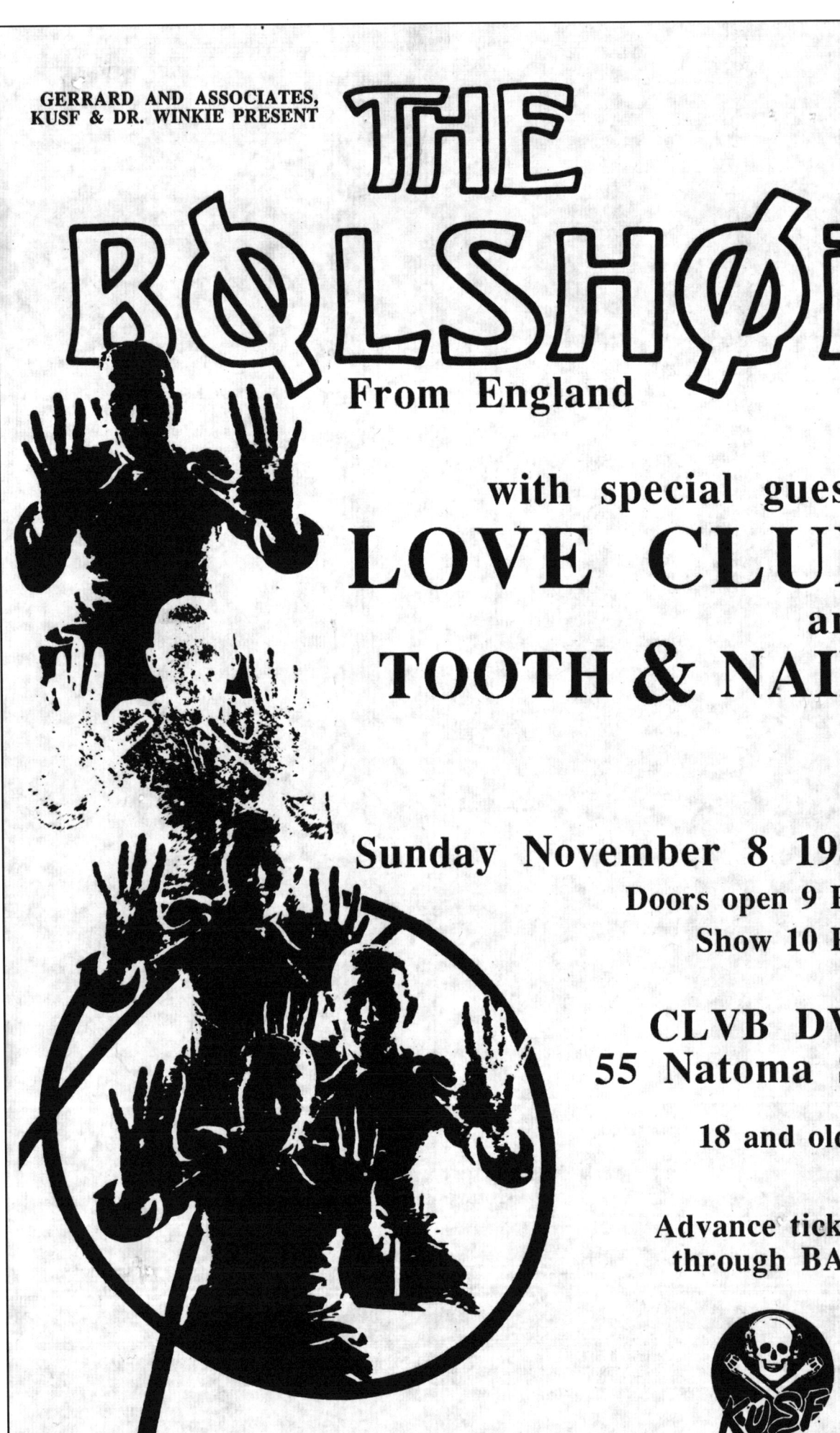

JULY
GOTTA WANNA

11, 12 QT
1312 Polk

18 VIS w/Murmurs
628 Divisadero Slantstep

25 THE OMNI w/Fishbone
4799 Shattuck, Oakland

FOR BOOKING 665-9091

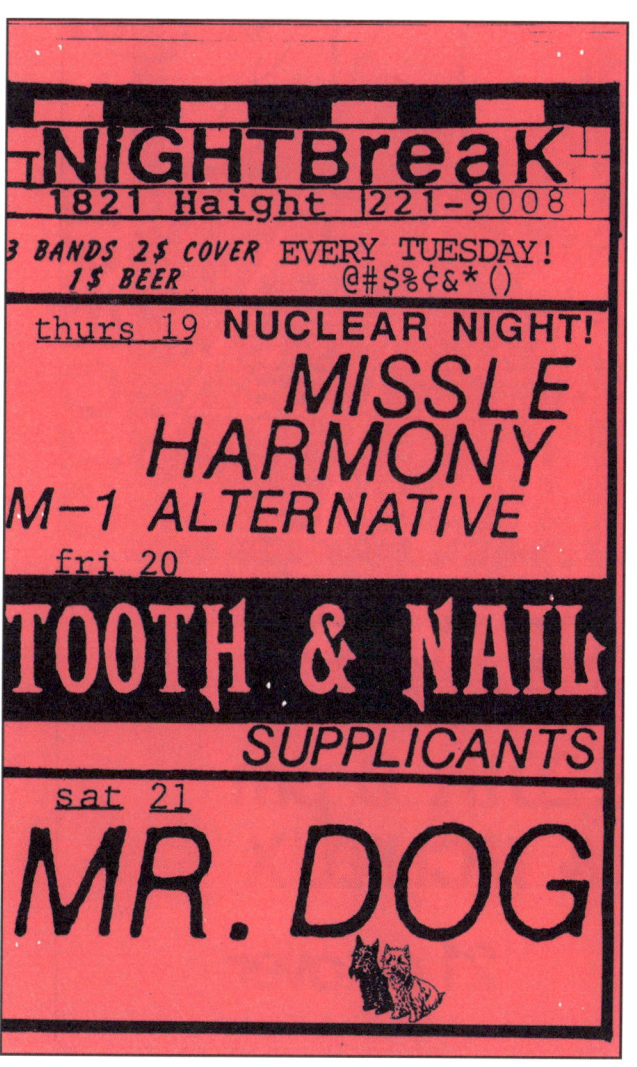

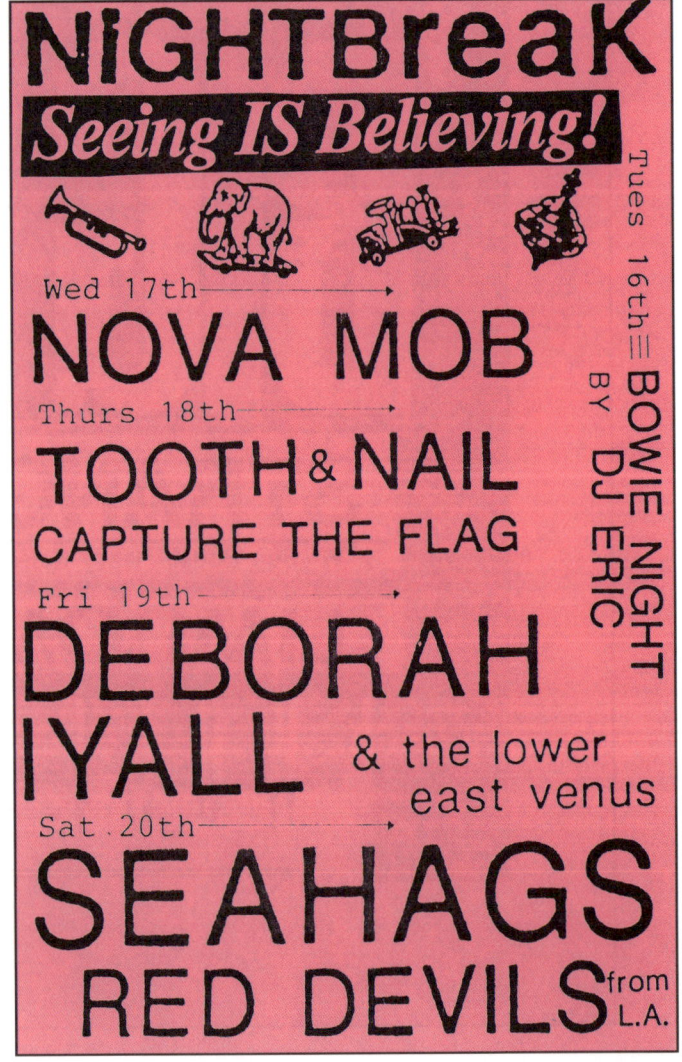

MONKEY RHYTHM

9:00 PM	Saturday, August 3	STONE, SF
	Friday, August 9	NIGHTBREAK, SF

with

FREAKY EXECUTIVES

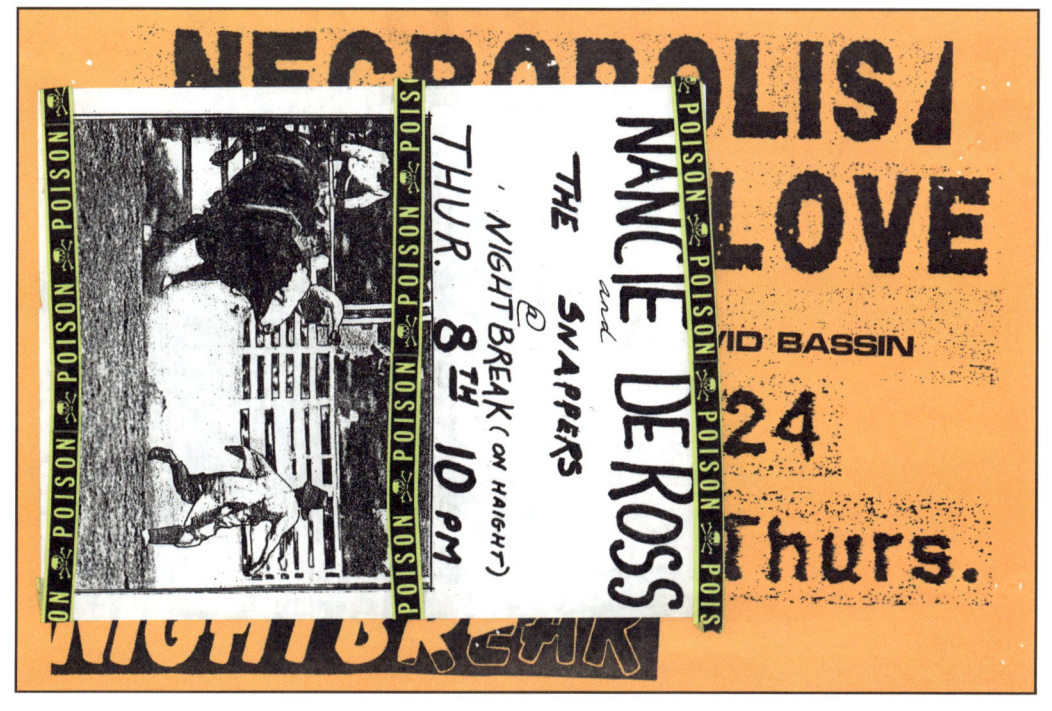

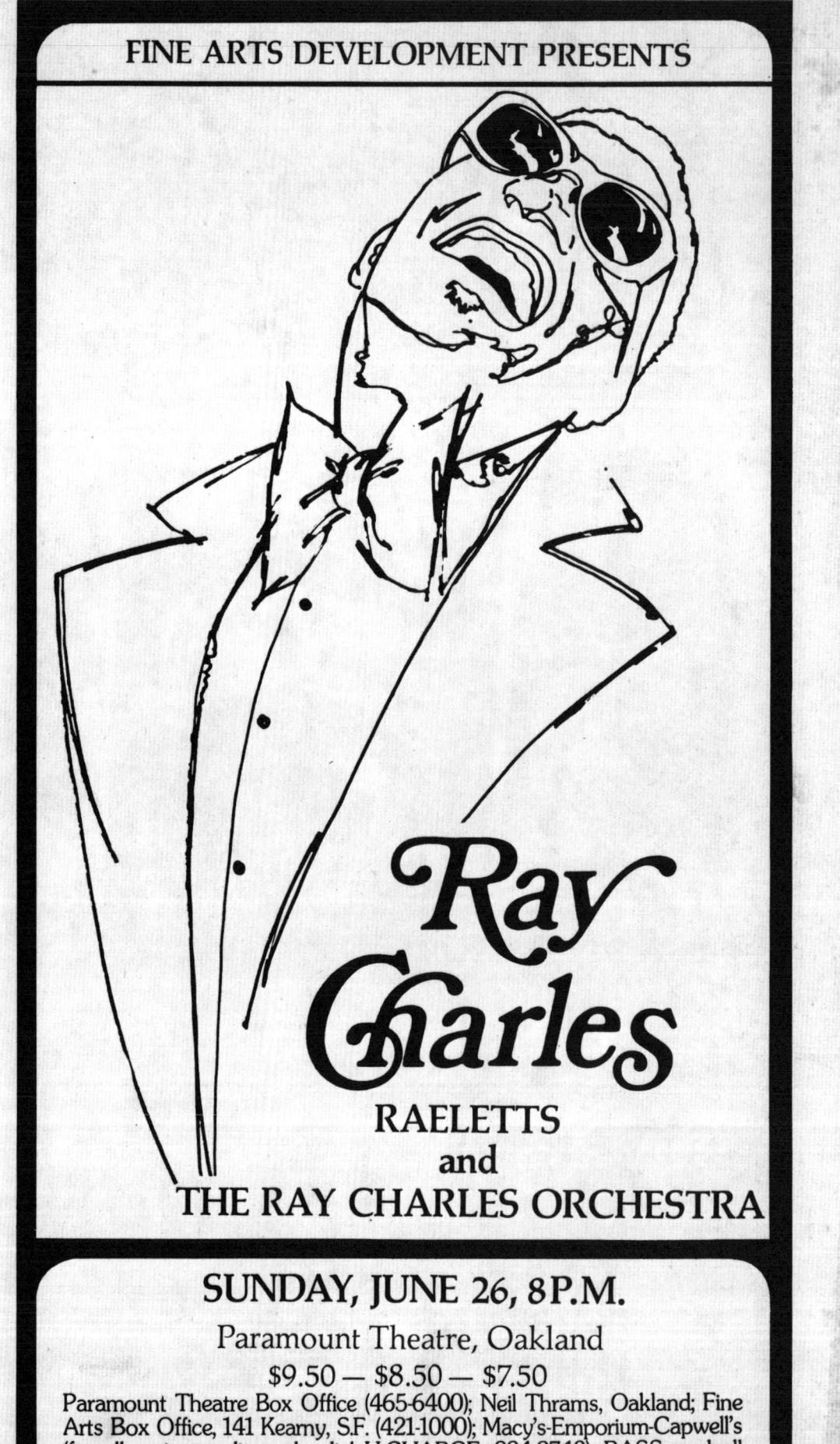

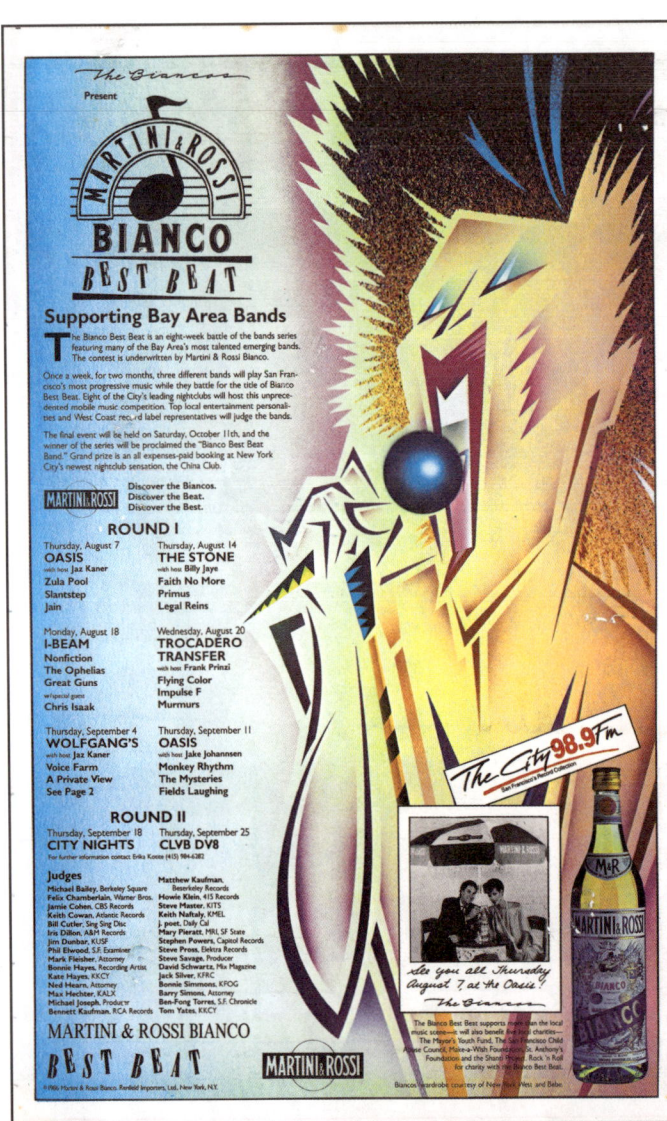

FOLK CONCERT
K　　A　　L　　X

PRESENTS

The Washington Squares
Bob Gibson
The Muskrats
Phranc

Thursday, October 24th   8 p.m.
Wheeler Auditorium, U.C. Berkeley

Tickets Available At:
Cal Performance Box Office
101 Zellerbach Hall
(415) 642-9988

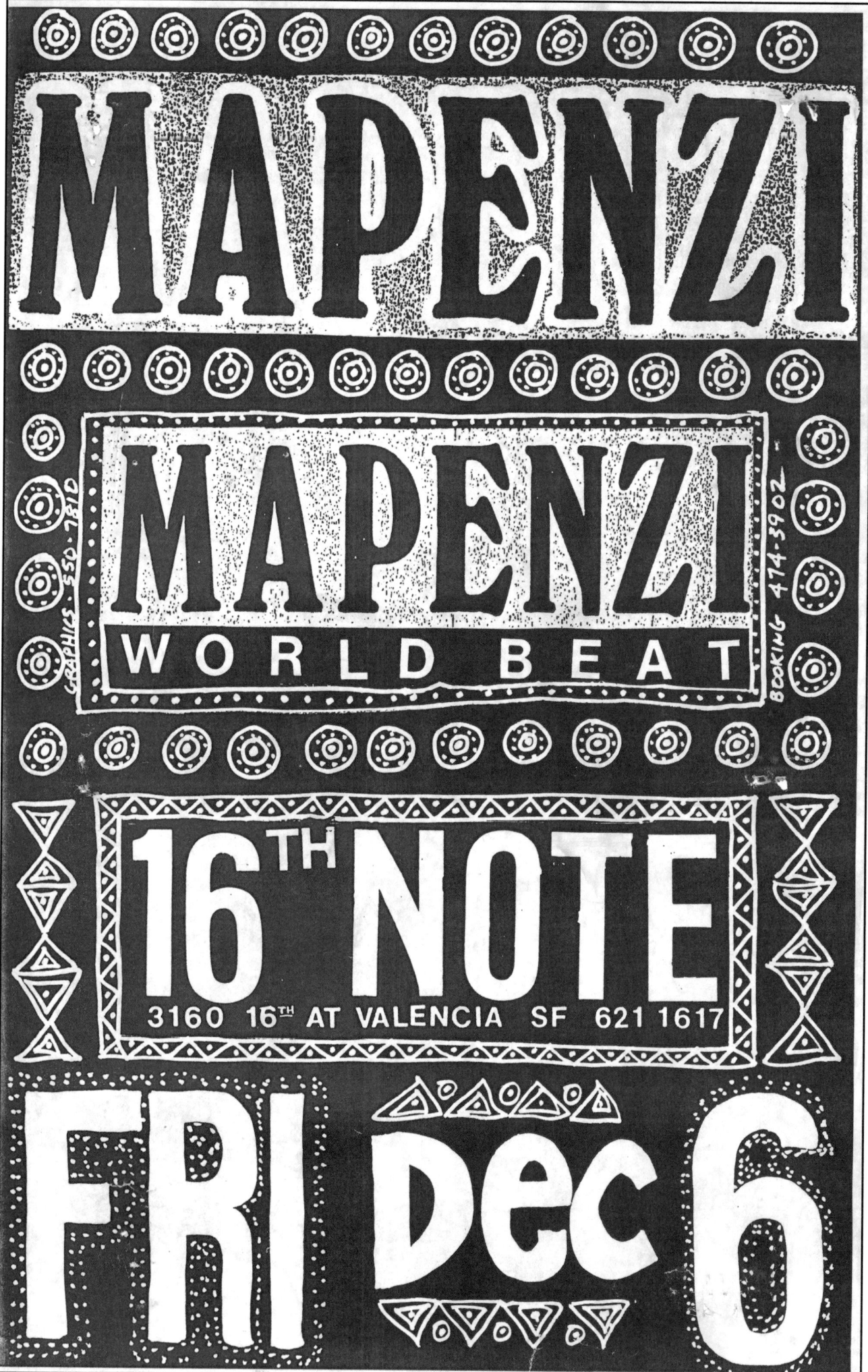

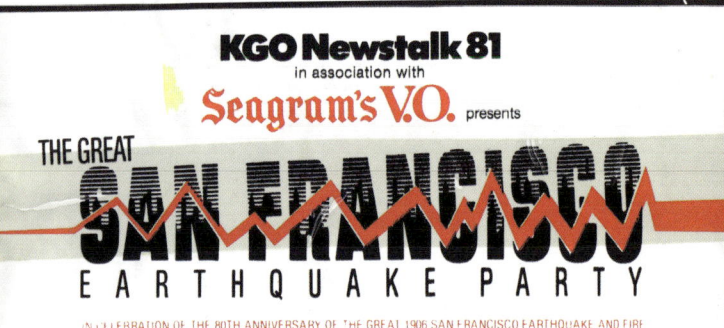

KGO Newstalk 81
in association with
Seagram's V.O. presents

THE GREAT SAN FRANCISCO EARTHQUAKE PARTY

IN CELEBRATION OF THE 80TH ANNIVERSARY OF THE GREAT 1906 SAN FRANCISCO EARTHQUAKE AND FIRE

Friday, April 18, 1986 — 7:00 p.m.
San Francisco Civic Auditorium

Don't Miss the Ultimate Dance Party!

ZASU PITTS MEMORIAL ORCHESTRA
FREAKY EXECUTIVES
SHARON McNIGHT

PRIDE AND JOY   TOMMIE

PLUS SURPRISE GUESTS!

★ "Streets of San Francisco" Food and Libations Alley
★ Re-Creation of the 1906 Earthquake and Fire
★ Multi-Media Program in Lights, Sound and Special Effects

ADMISSION $15.00

TICKETS AVAILABLE AT BASS TICKET CENTERS INCLUDING RECORD FACTORY
CHARGE BY PHONE (415) 762-BASS
(408) 998-BASS • (916) 395-BASS
(707) 762-BASS • (209) 466-BASS

THE EIGHTIETH ANNIVERSARY OF THE GREAT SAN FRANCISCO EARTHQUAKE & FIRE 1906-1986

Proceeds to Benefit AIDS Research at
The City of Hope National Medical Center

City of Hope • 657 Mission Street • San Francisco • 981-HOPE

Posters to be removed by April 20, 1986

 City of Hope

TRAGIC MULATTO
FUCK BUBBLE
VOMIT LAUNCH

August 1   Hotel Utah

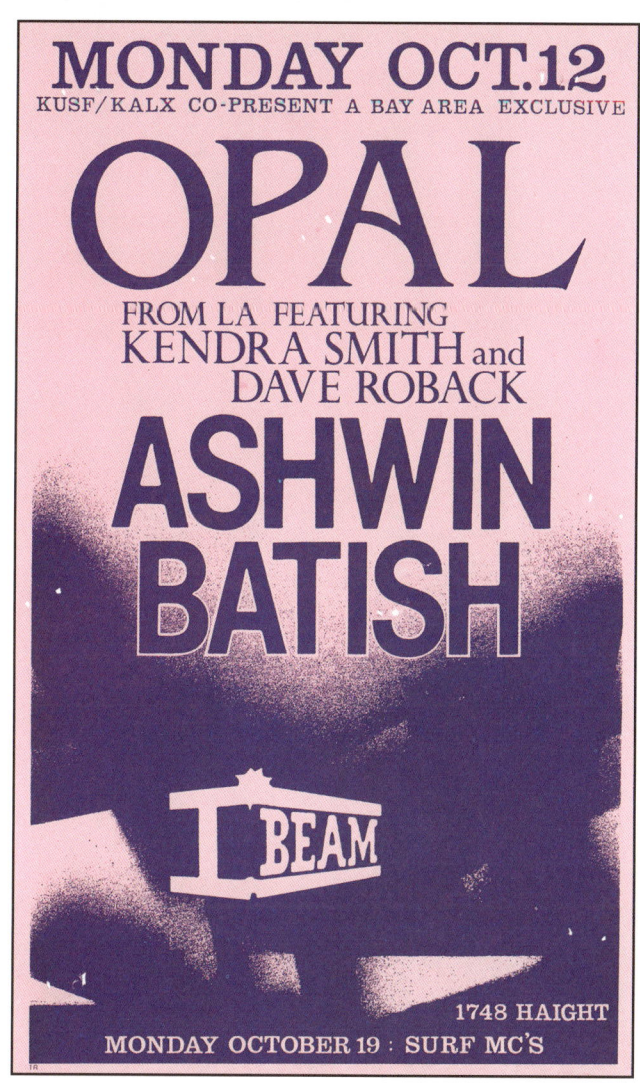

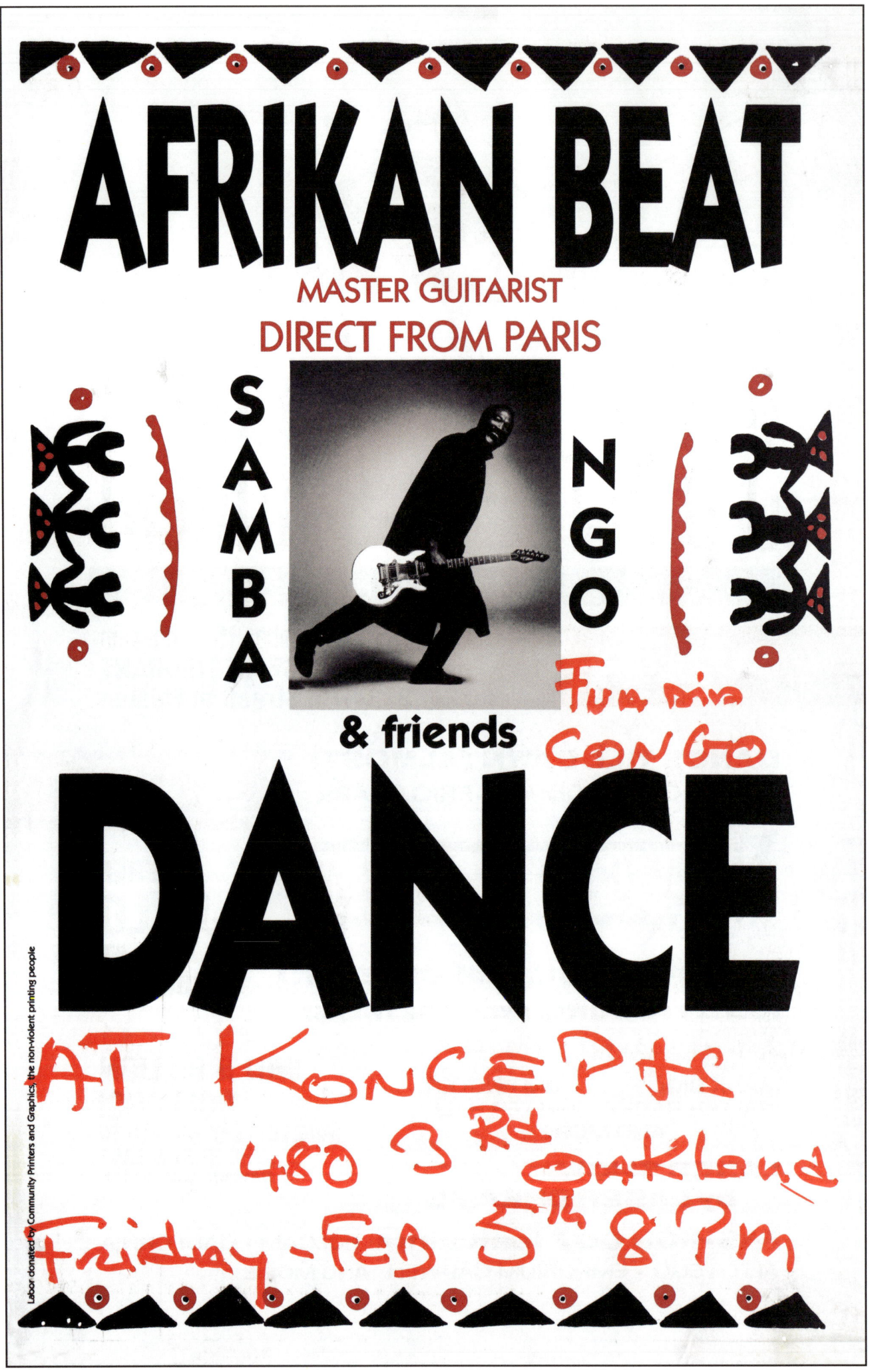

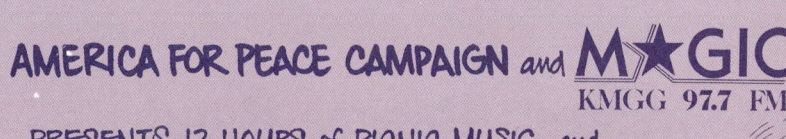

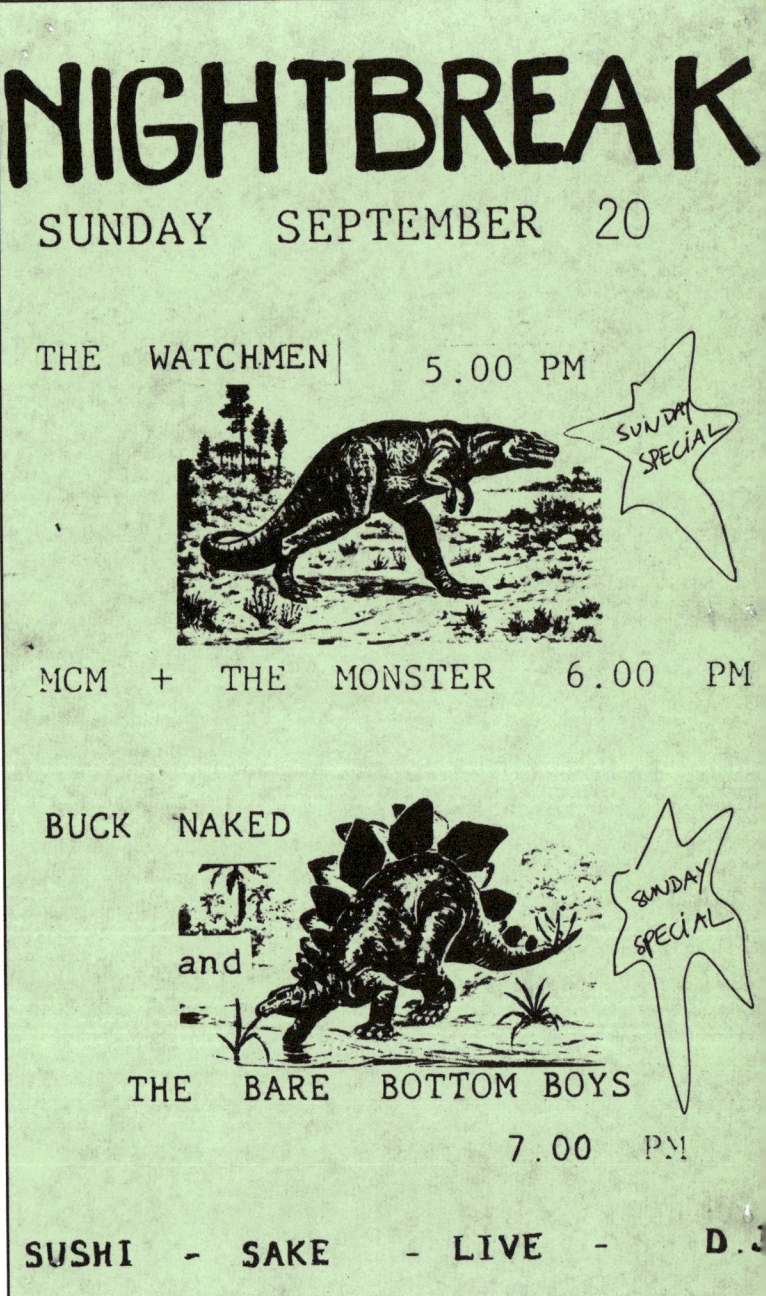

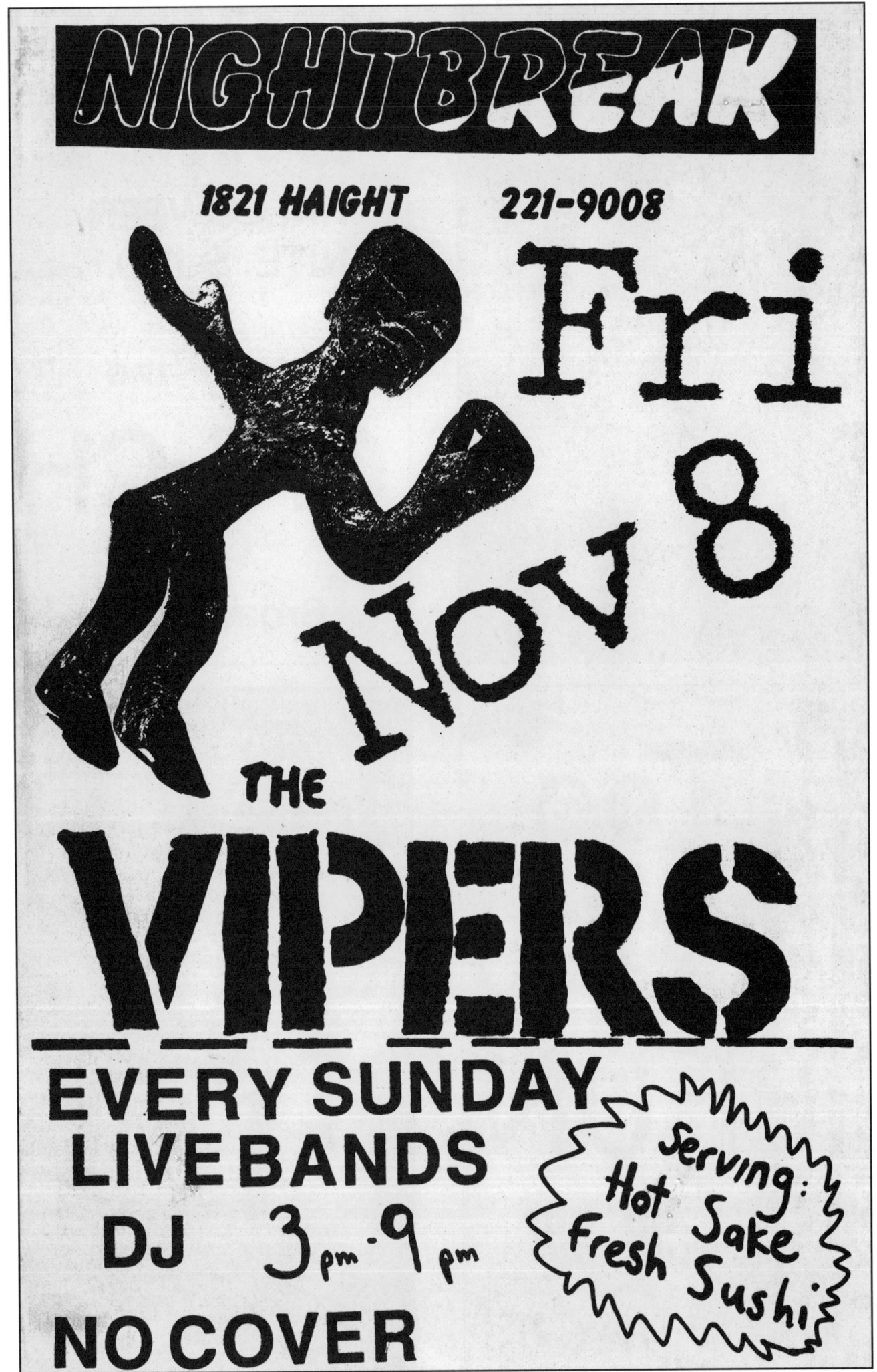

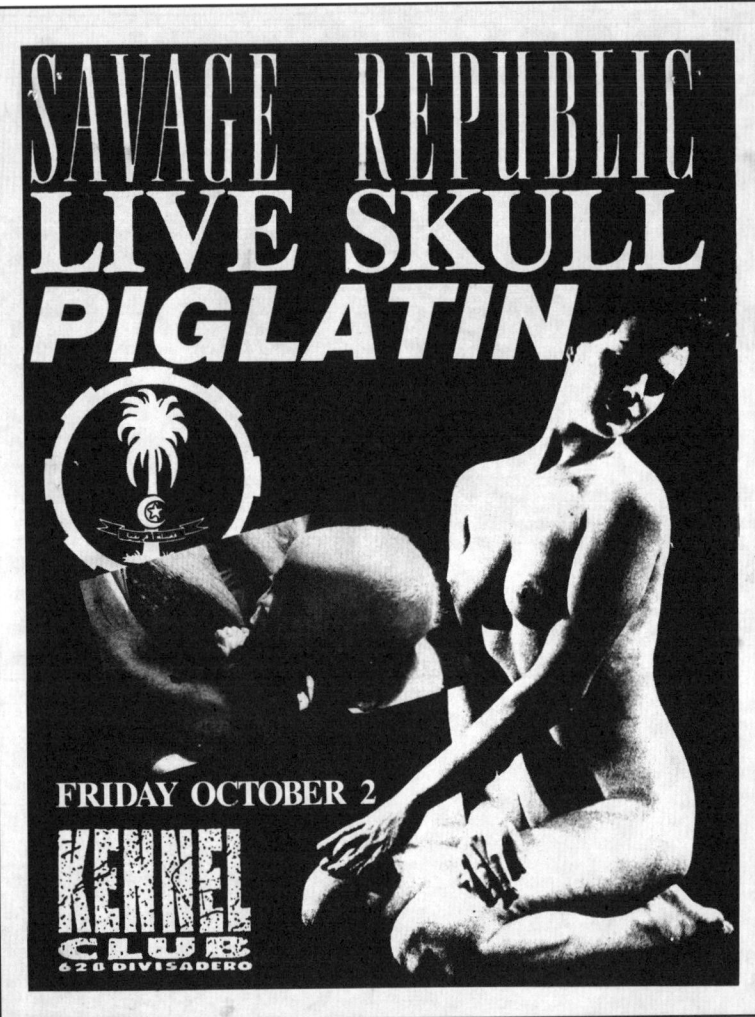

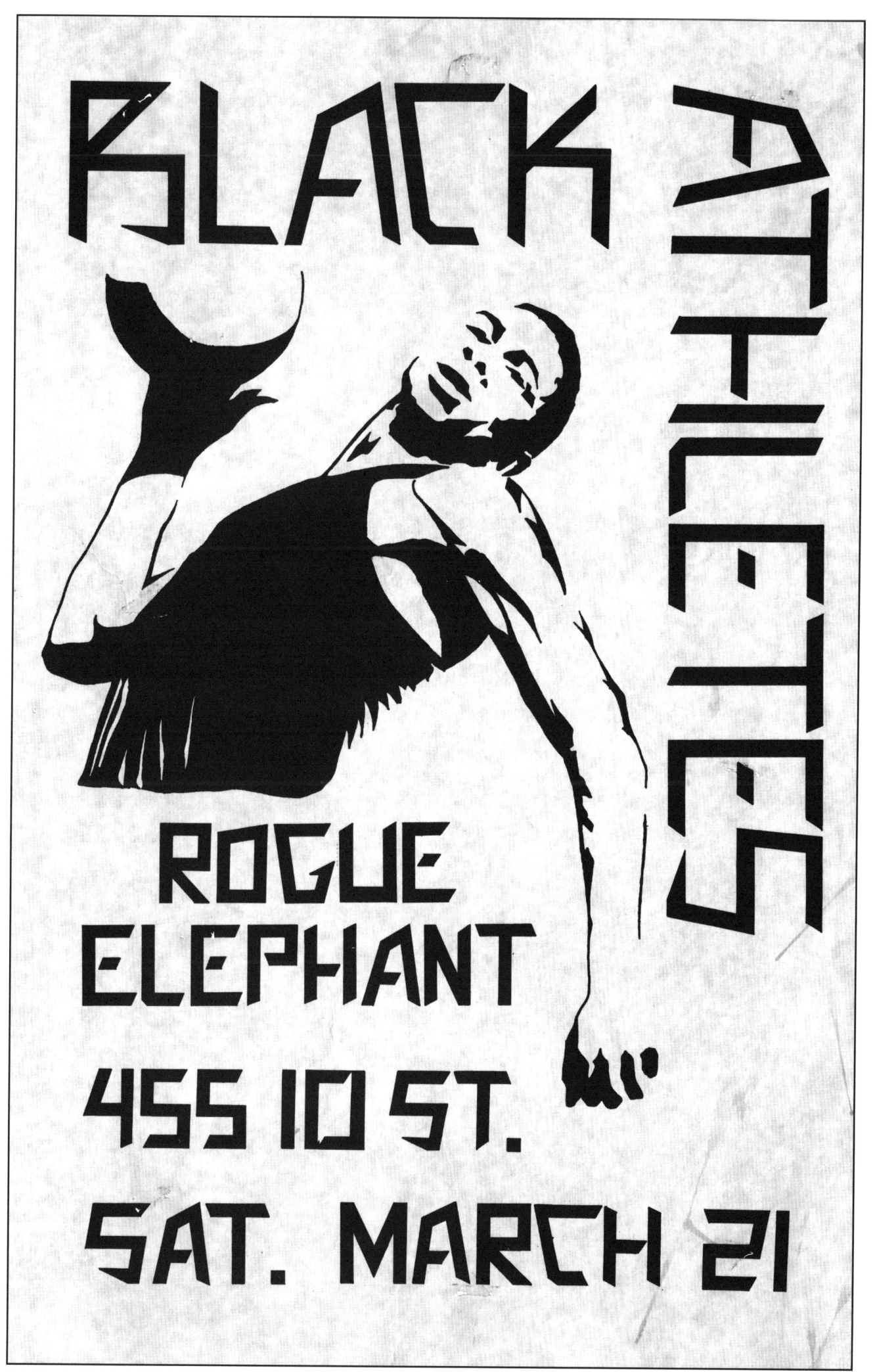

FREAKY EXECUTIVES
SAT – AUG 3
THE STONE

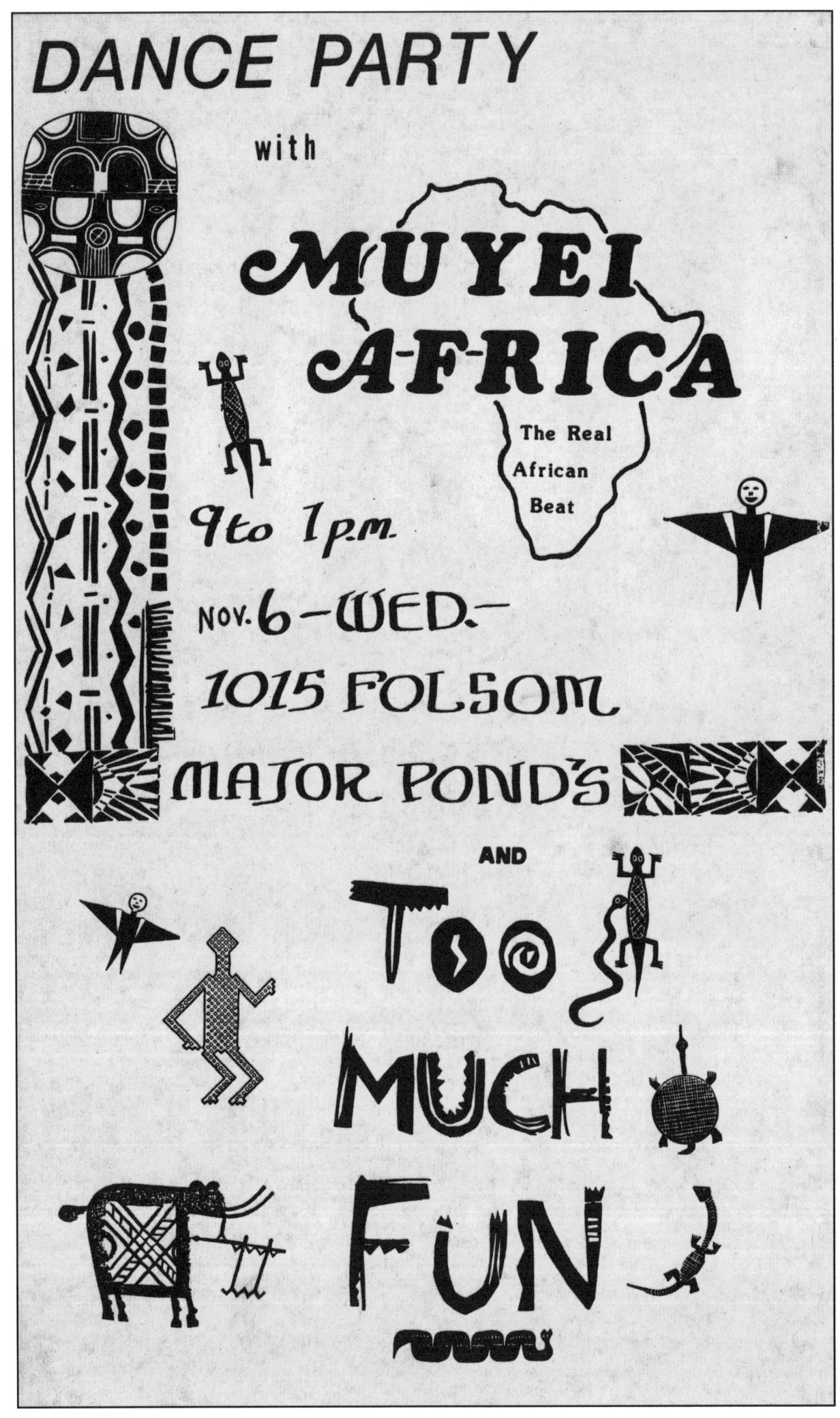

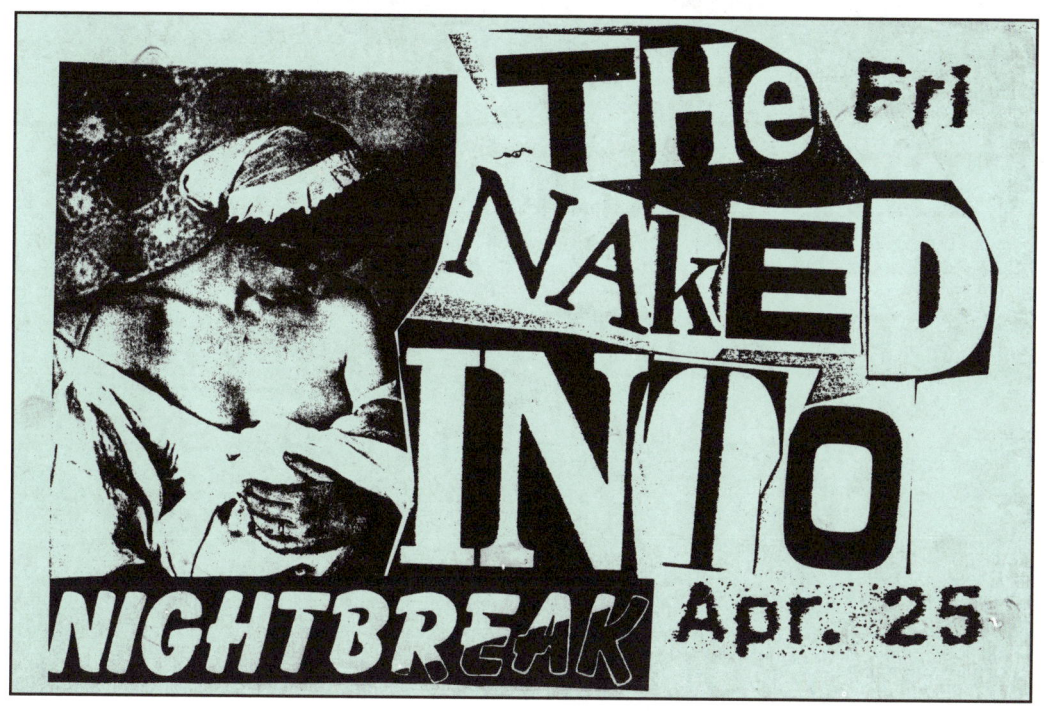

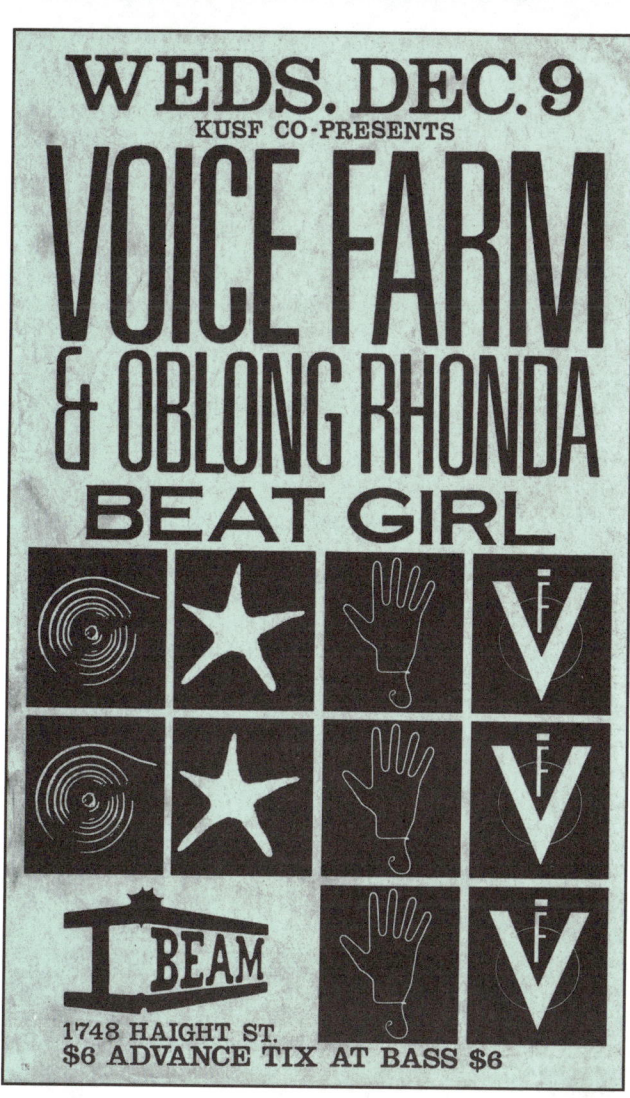

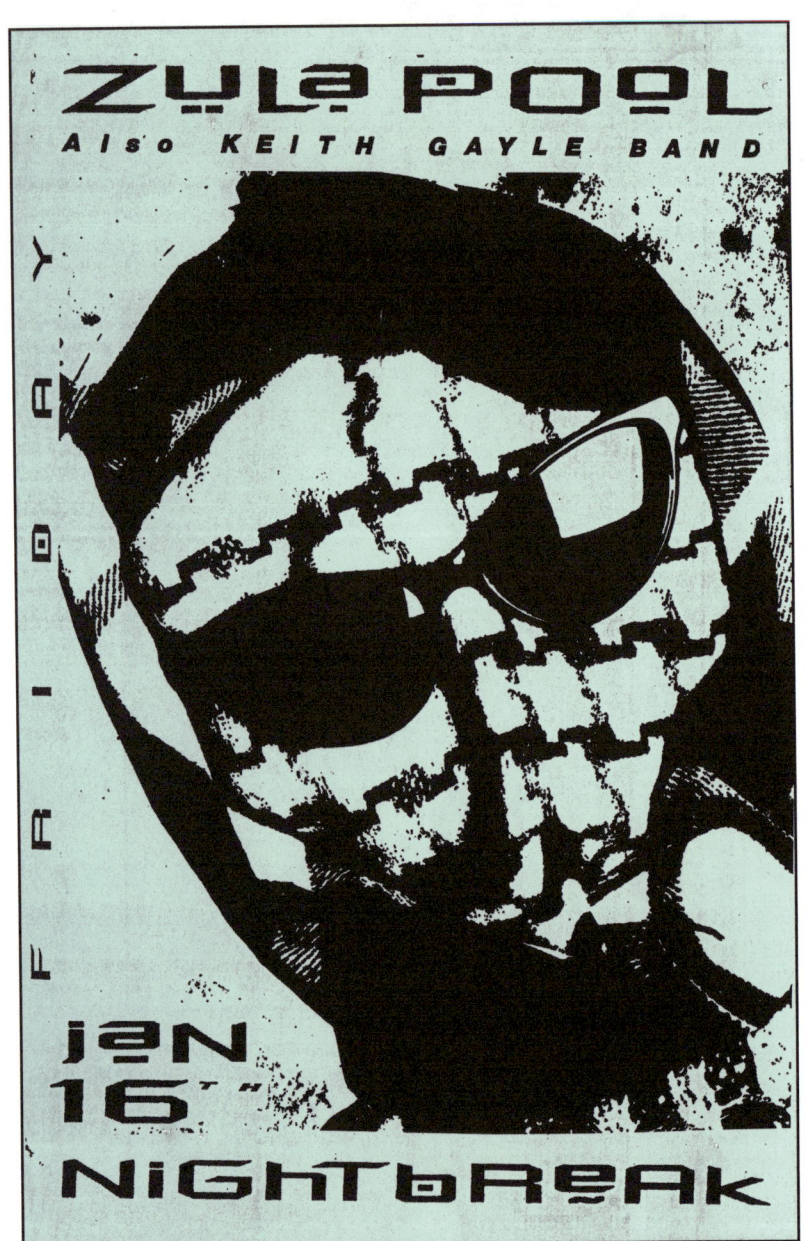

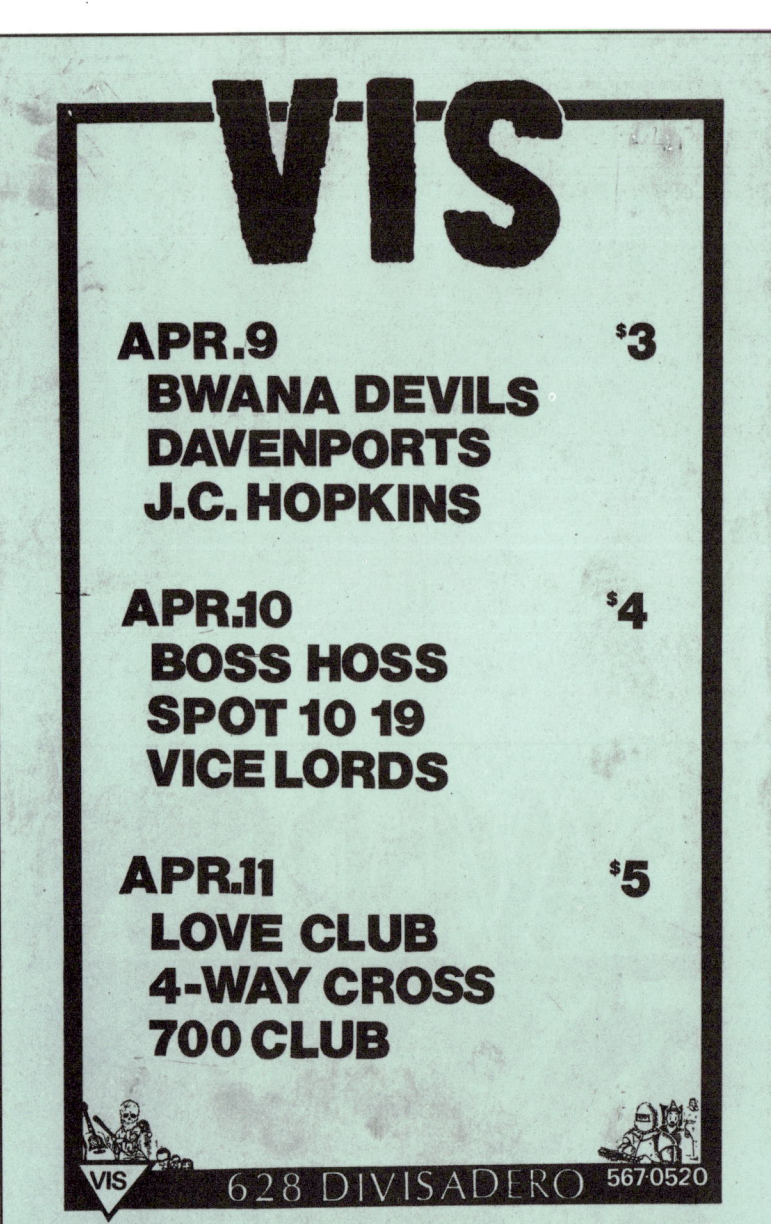

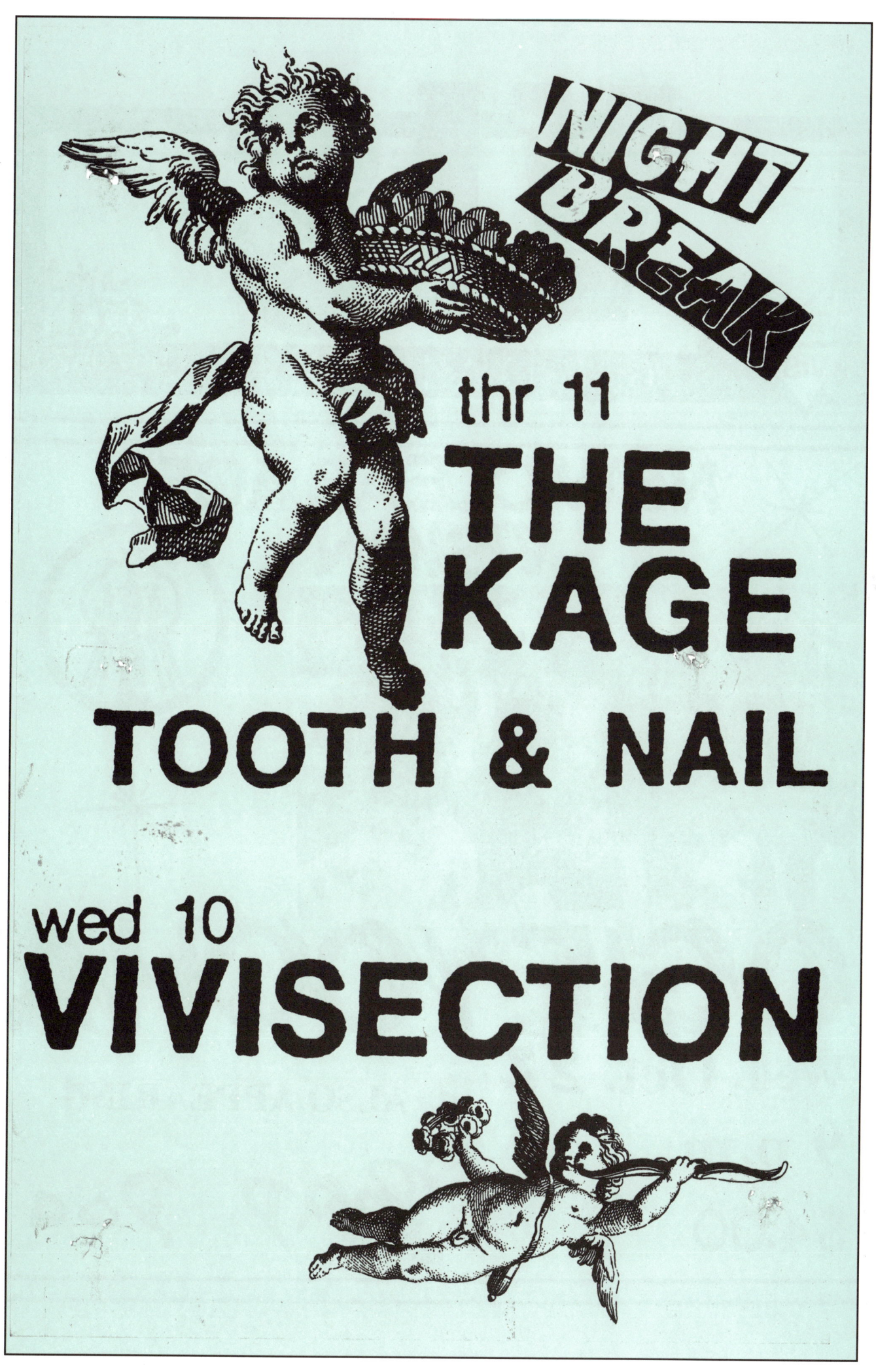

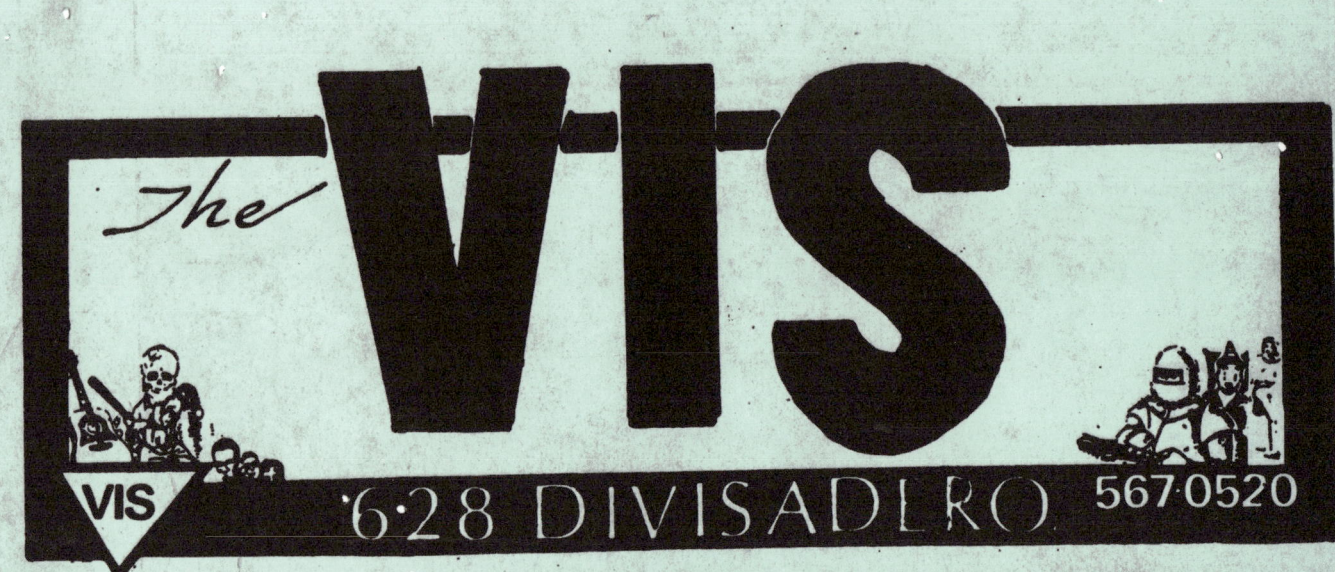

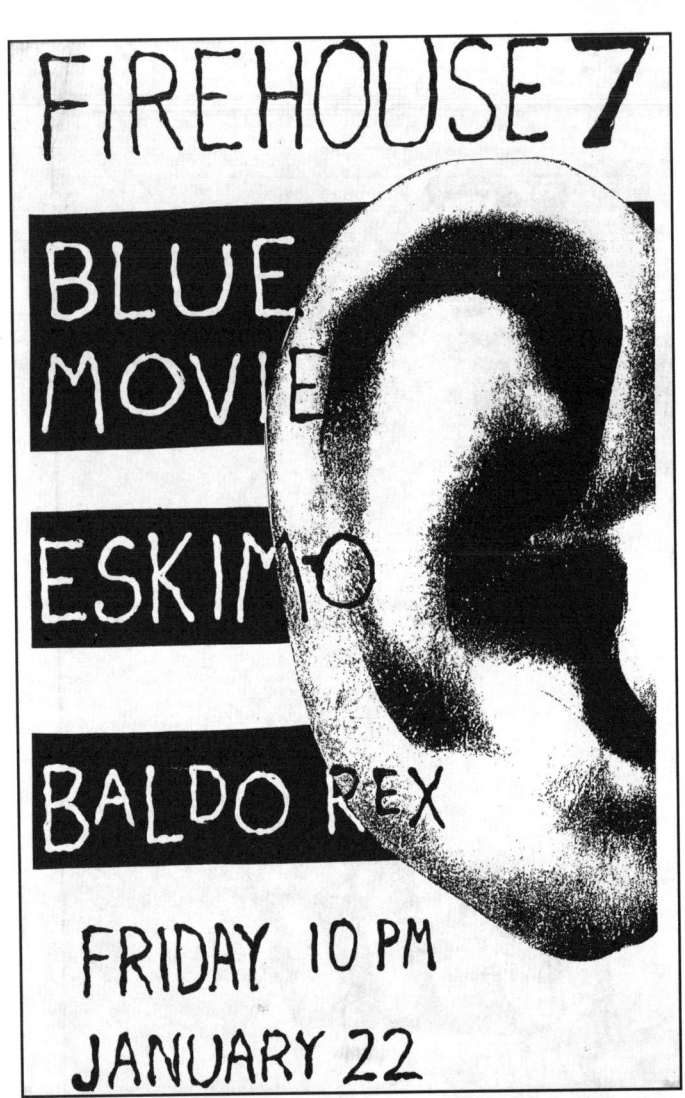

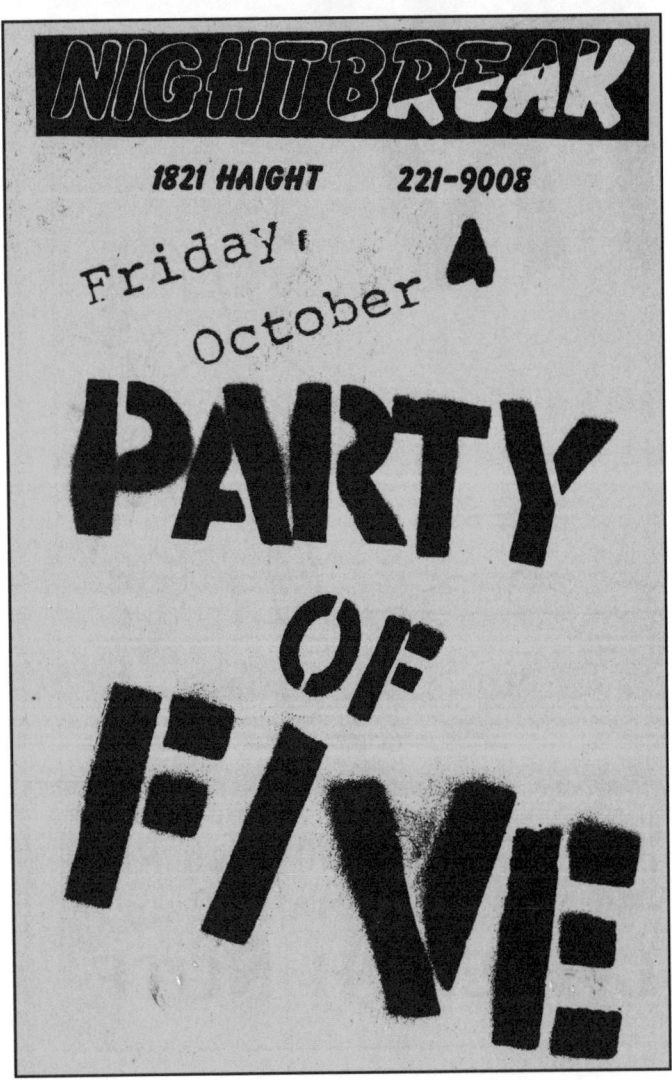

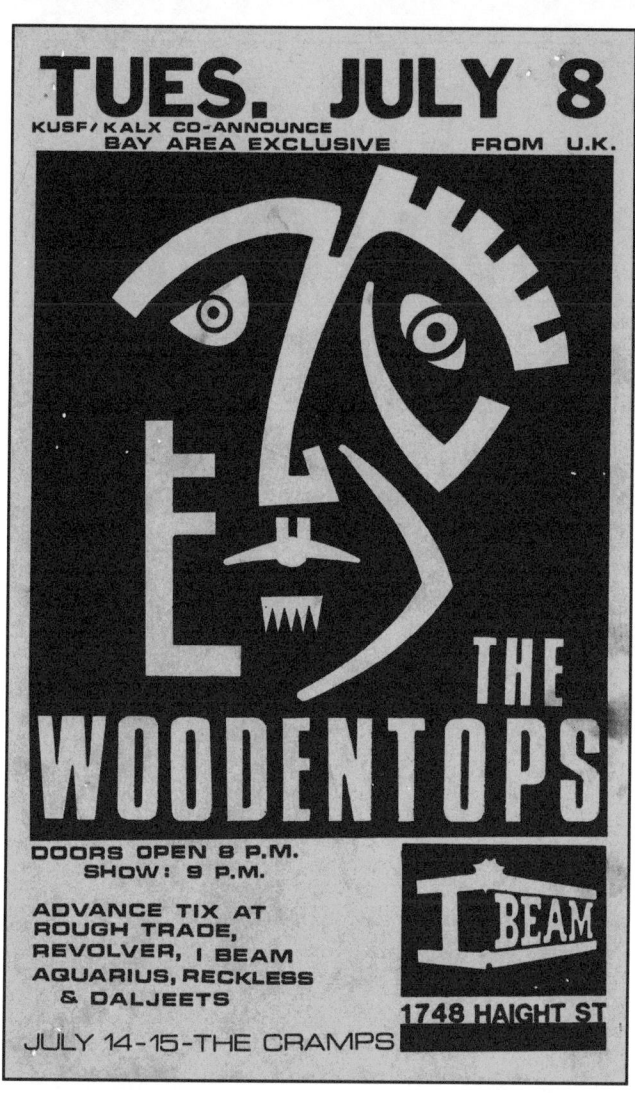

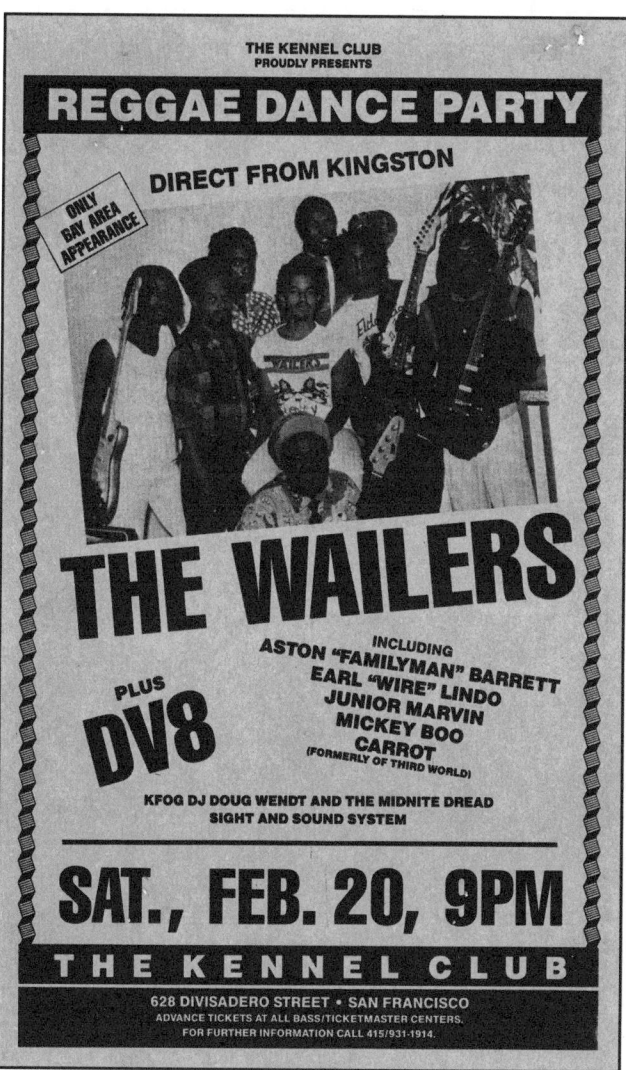
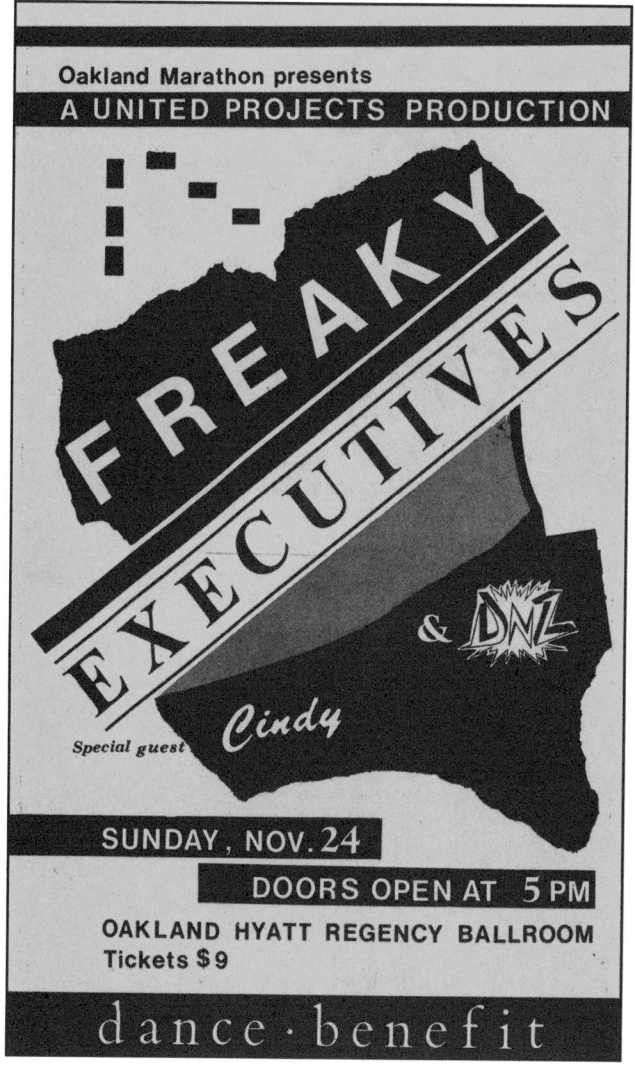

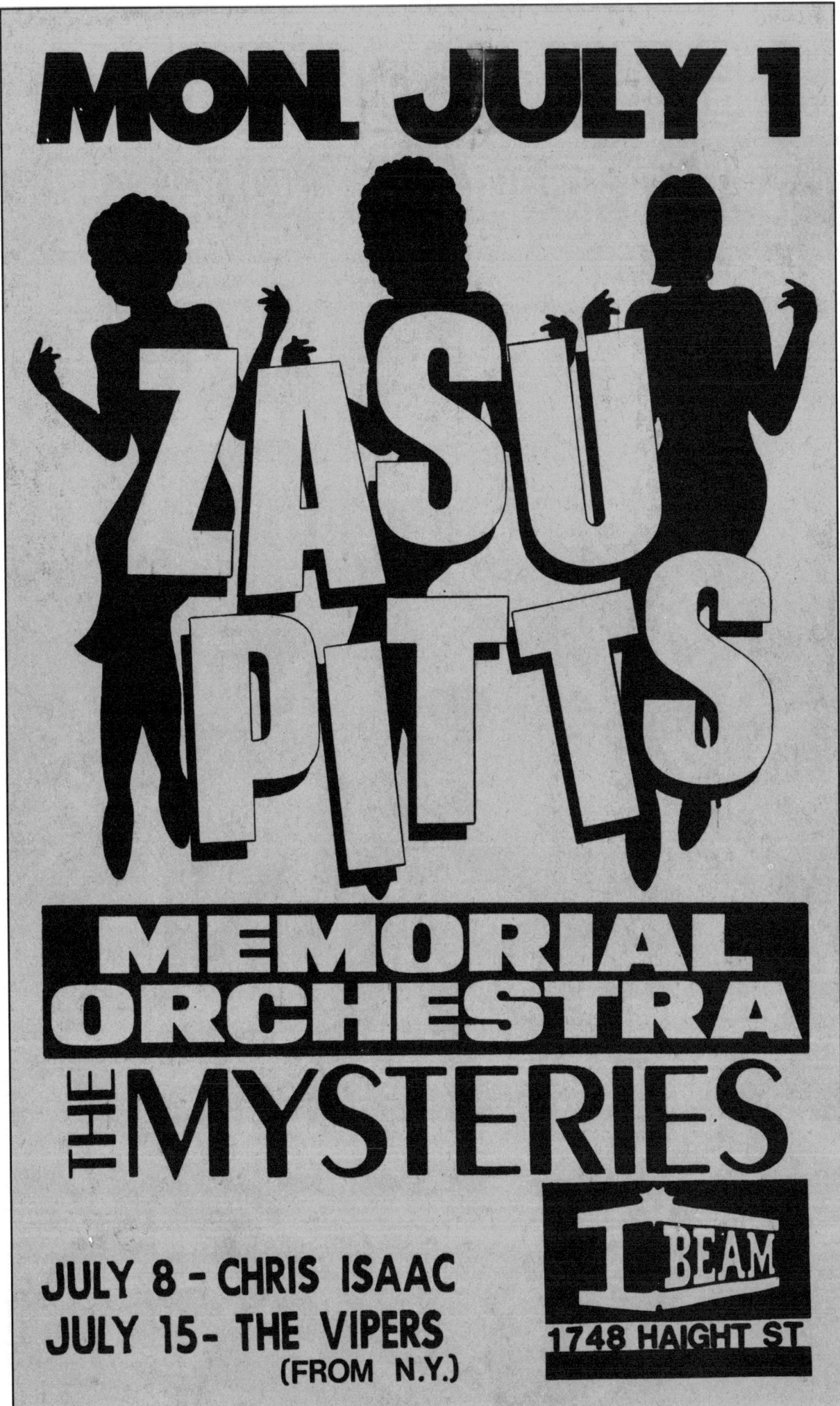

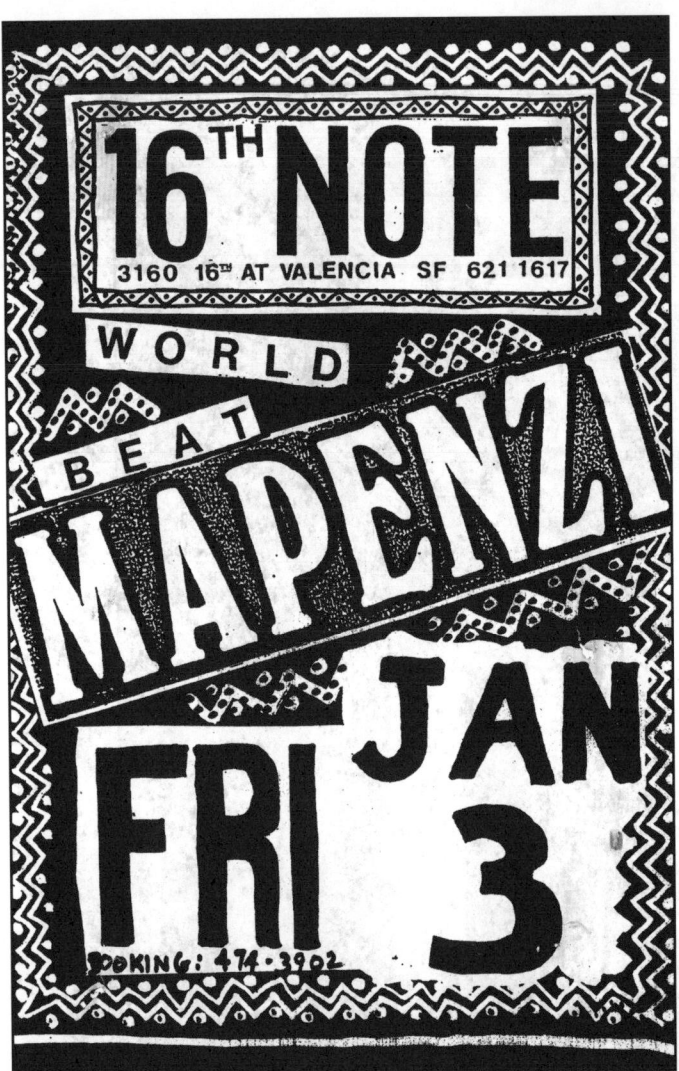

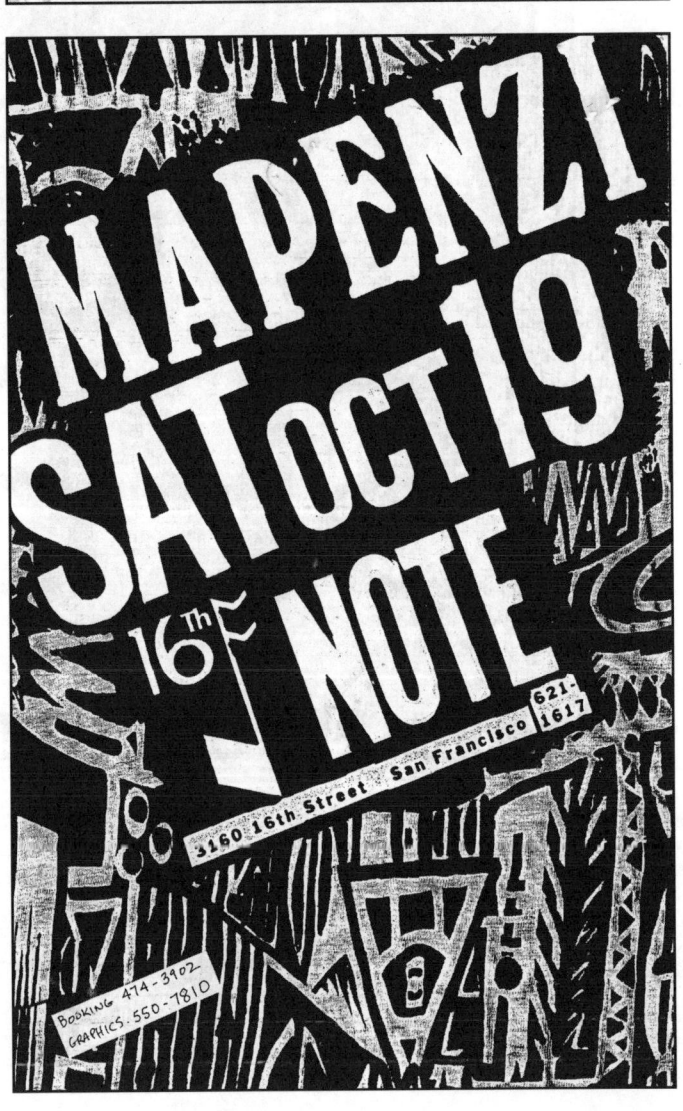

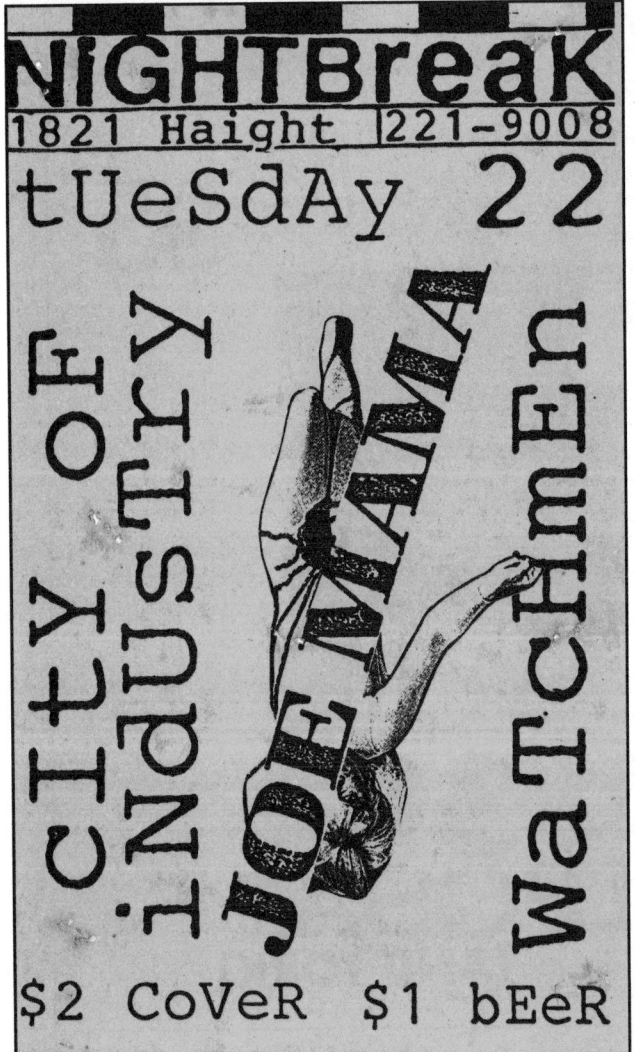

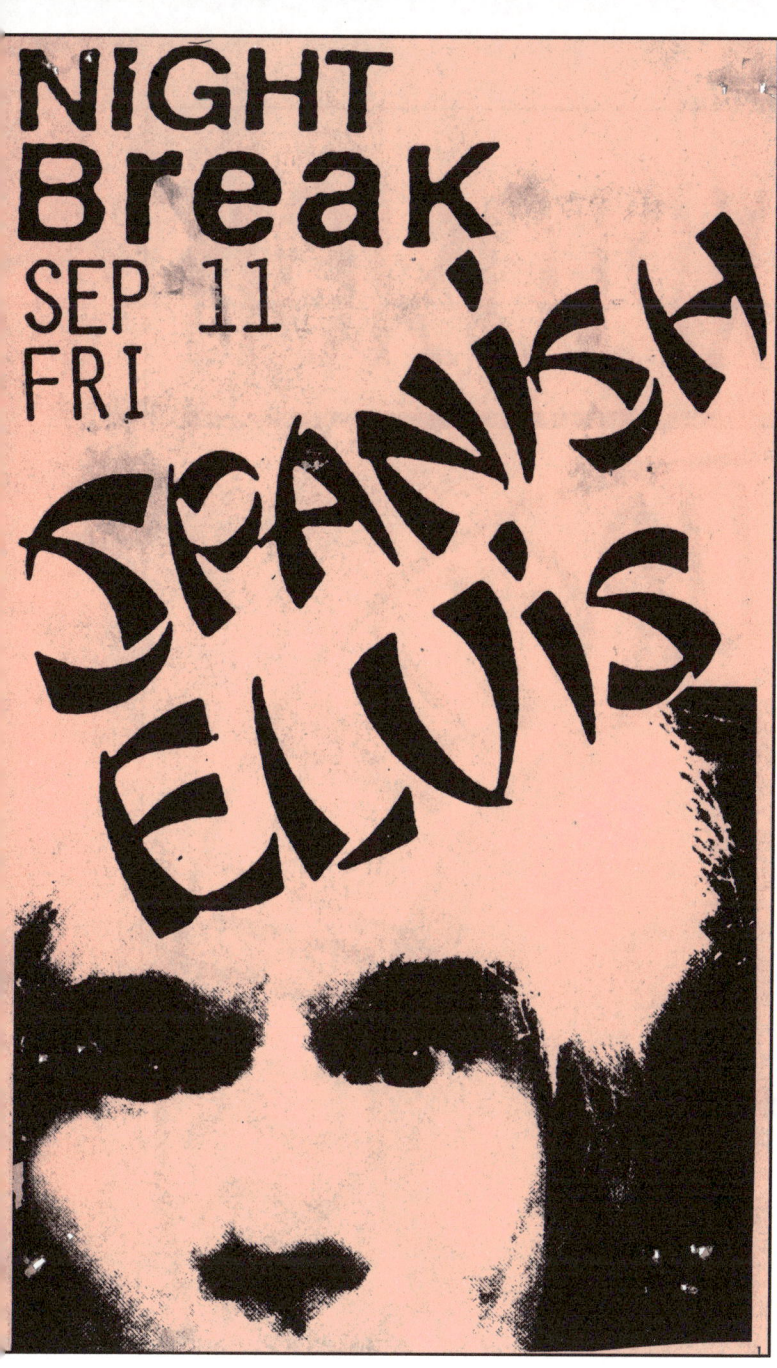

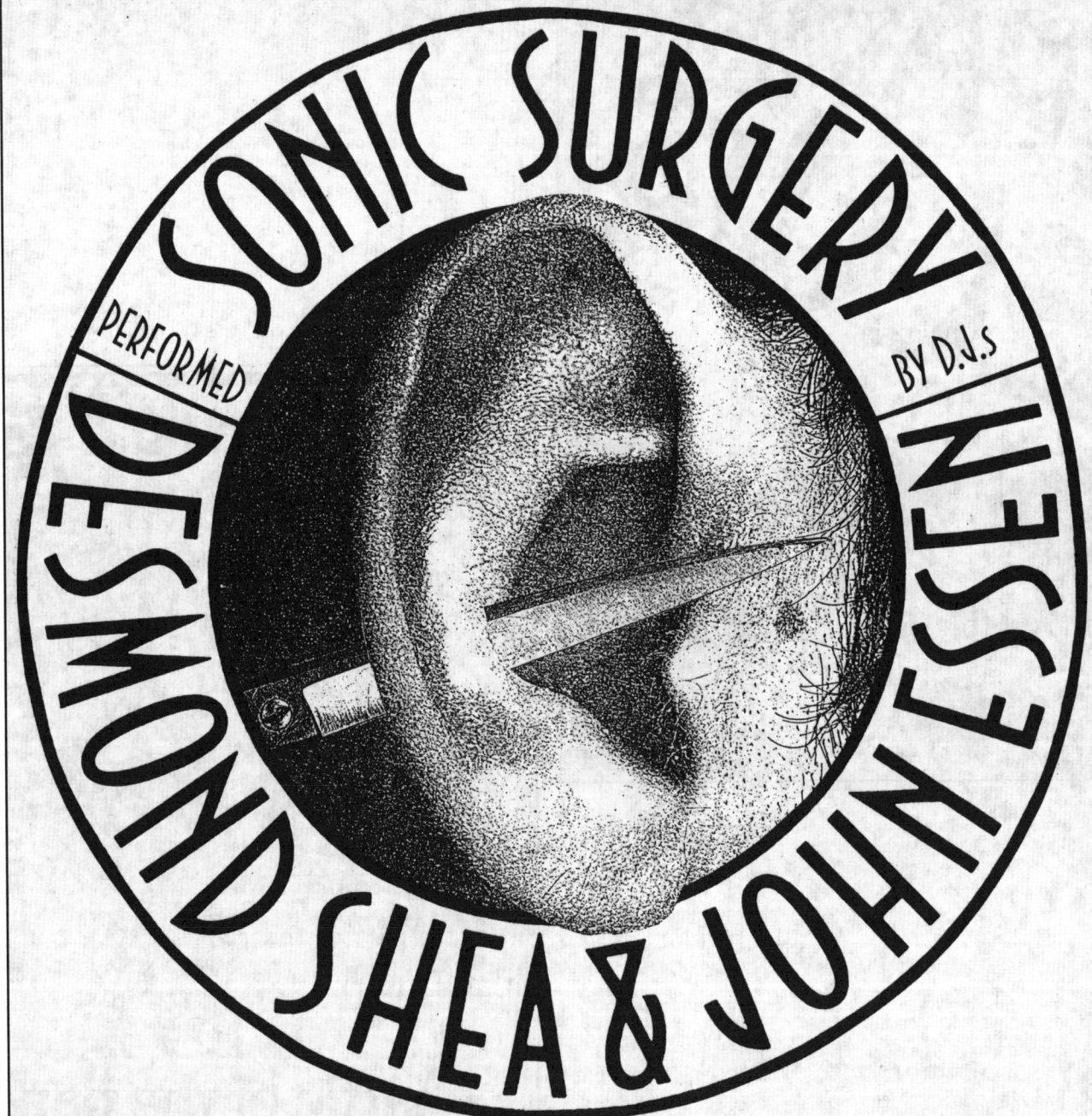

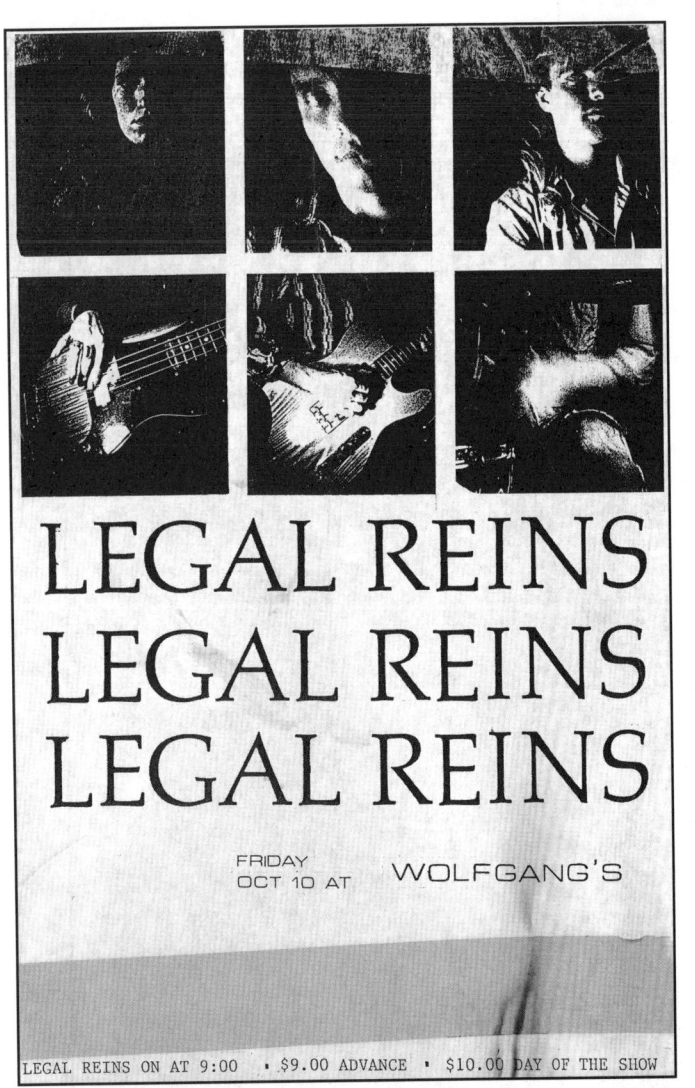

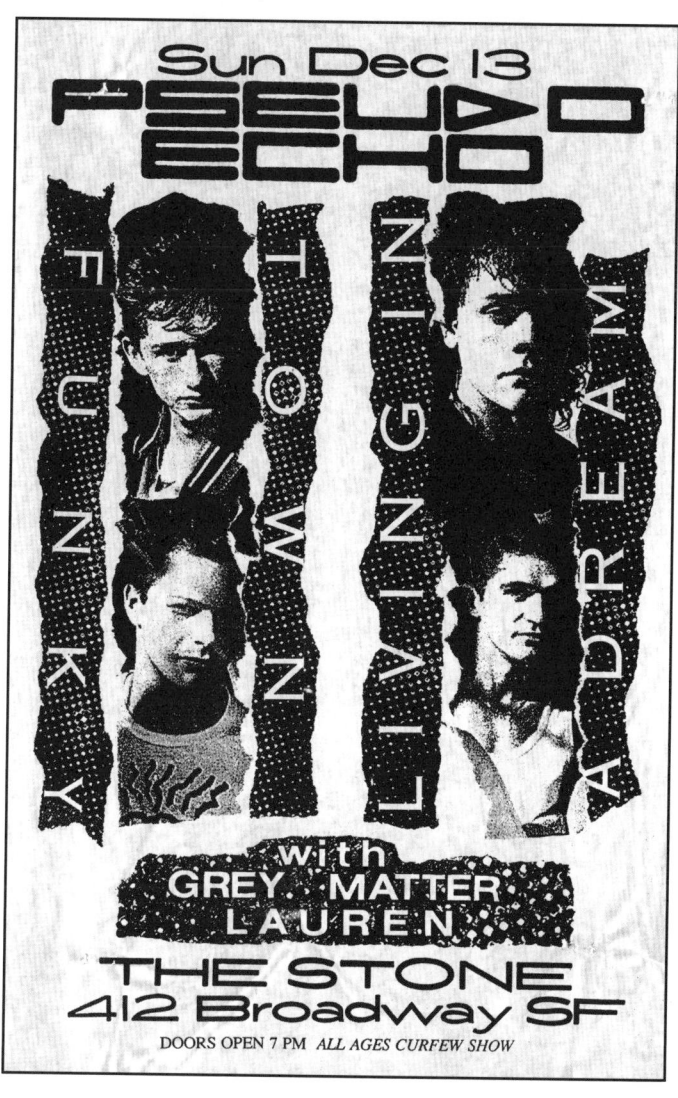
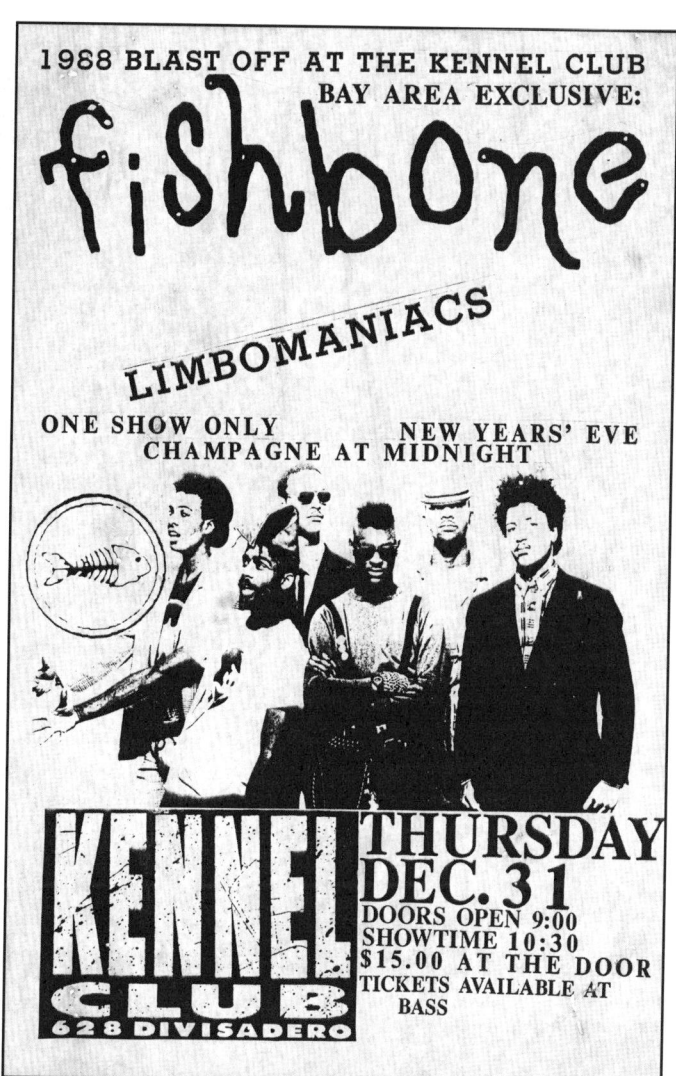

the Friends of Stephen Bingham Defense Com.

BIG CITY and the LOOTERS in a WORLD BEAT DANCE BENEFIT for stephen BINGHAM

Stephen Bingham is the Bay Area attorney charged with conspiracy and murder in the August 21, 1971 events at San Quentin that left prison leader George Jackson and five others dead.

He is innocent of these charges, and goes on trial in Marin Court Superior Court in January 1986 to gain his acquittal.

FRI. OCT. 25, 1985
9pm $7.00 at the FARM
1499 Potrero Ave. S.F.
INFO - 861-0202

MISSION GRÁFICA 85

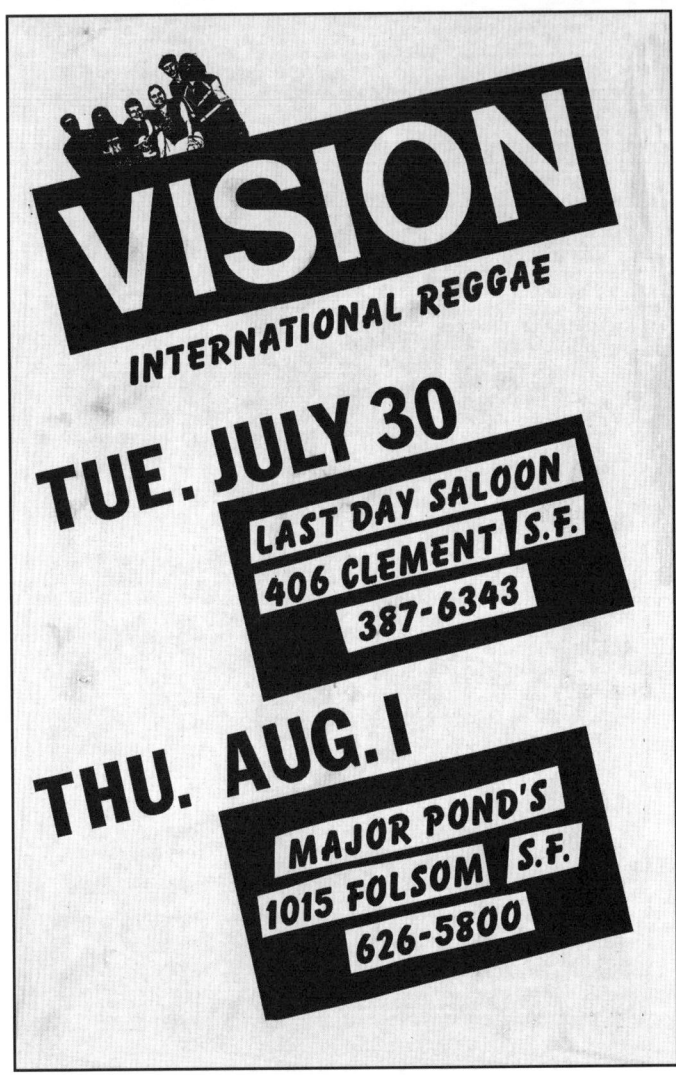

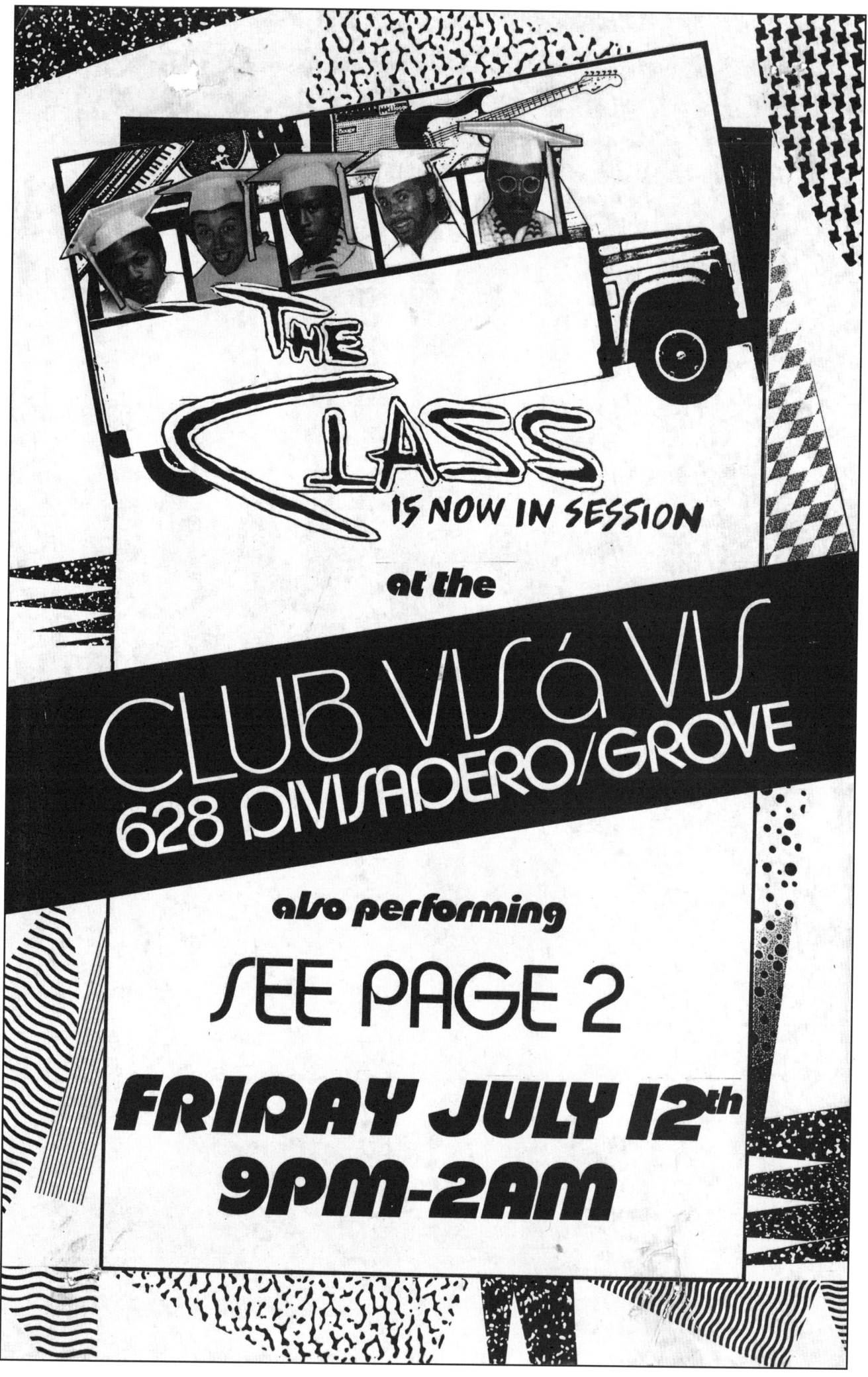

Too Much Fun

TUESDAY

AUGUST 6TH

WARRIORS of the BEAT

LAST DAY SALOON

406 CLEMENT — 9 PM – 1 AM

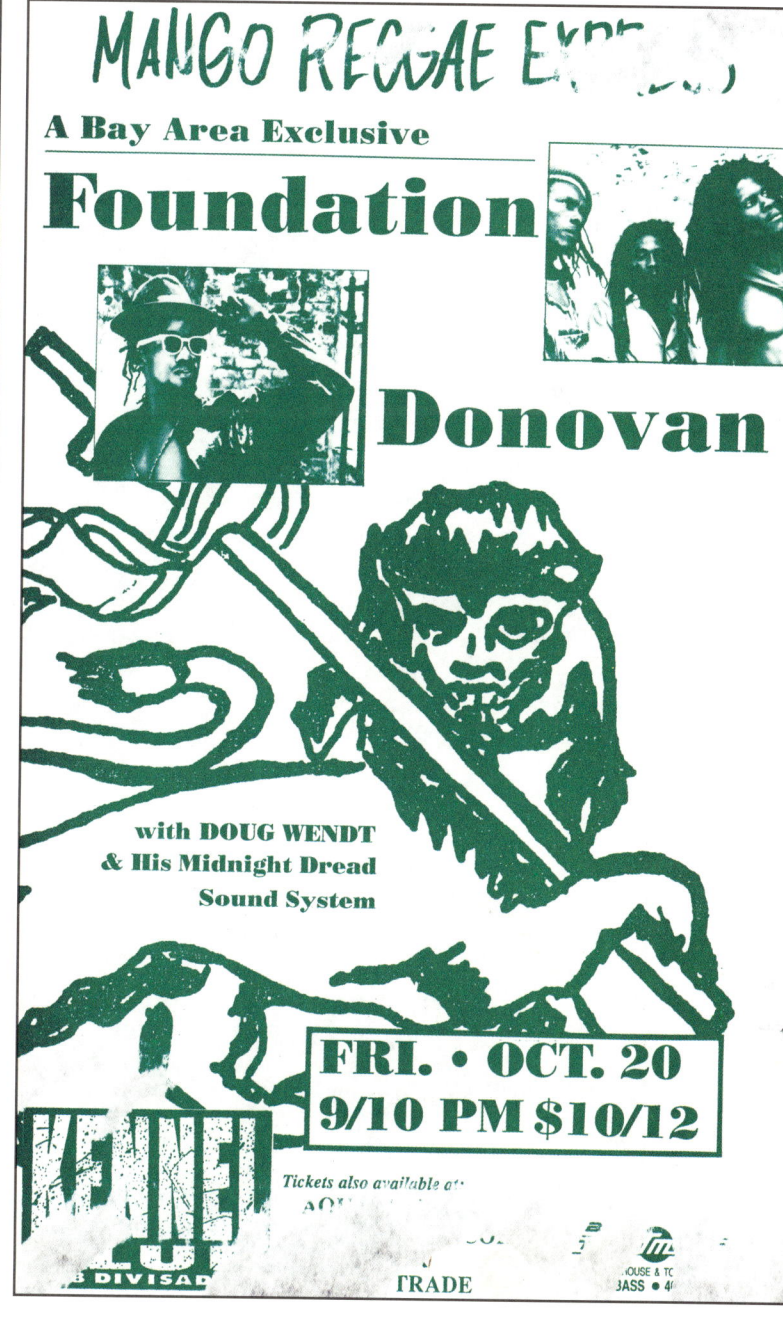

TO DEVELOP THE EDUCATIONAL AND CULTURAL EXCHANGE PROGRAM

RASTAFARI FOUNDATION
BENEFIT DANCE

THURS JUNE 19 1986 8PM

RAS MICHAEL SON'S OF NEGUS

RASKIDUS

WITH

SISTERS ZION   PRINCESS BAM BAM

PRINCE ITAL JOE

ALSO

AMBASSADOR RANKING

THE "BLACK EMPEROR" SOUND SYSTEM

AND

MC. SISTA CHEY KPOO

NONE PROFIT TAX DEDUCTIBLE
DONATION $10.00

TICKET AVAILABLE AT

TEN 4231- TELEGRAPH AVE OAKLAND CA.
PRINCE NEVILL'S RESTAURANT, 424 HAIGHT ST. S.F. CA.
CRIME OF FASHION, 678 HAIGHT ST., S.F. CA.
MARCUS BOOK STORE 1712 FILMORE. S.F. CA.
MARCUS BOOK STORE 3900 GROVE, ST. OAKLAND
ROUGH TRADE 326 SIXTH ST. S.F. CA.

RASKIDUS

PRINCE ITAL JOE

RAS MICHAEL

CESAR'S PALACE
3140 MISSION ST. SAN FRANCISCO
2 SETS OF TICKETS TO BE RAFFLED

WIN A TRIP FOR 2
TO JAMAICA   TO BELIZE

RAFFLE TICKET: DONATION $10 (need not be present)

SPONSORED BY

BELIZE INTERNATIONAL SOCCER ASSOCIATION

FOR TICKET'S INFORMATION

415-534-2132

THE HUNGRY MUST BE FED THE INFANTS CLOTHED THE ELDERLY PROTECTED

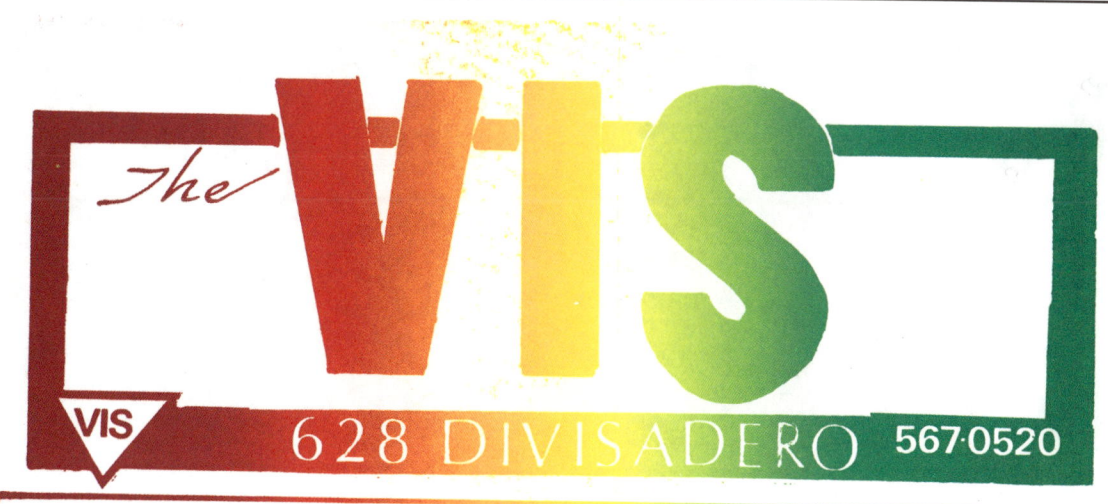

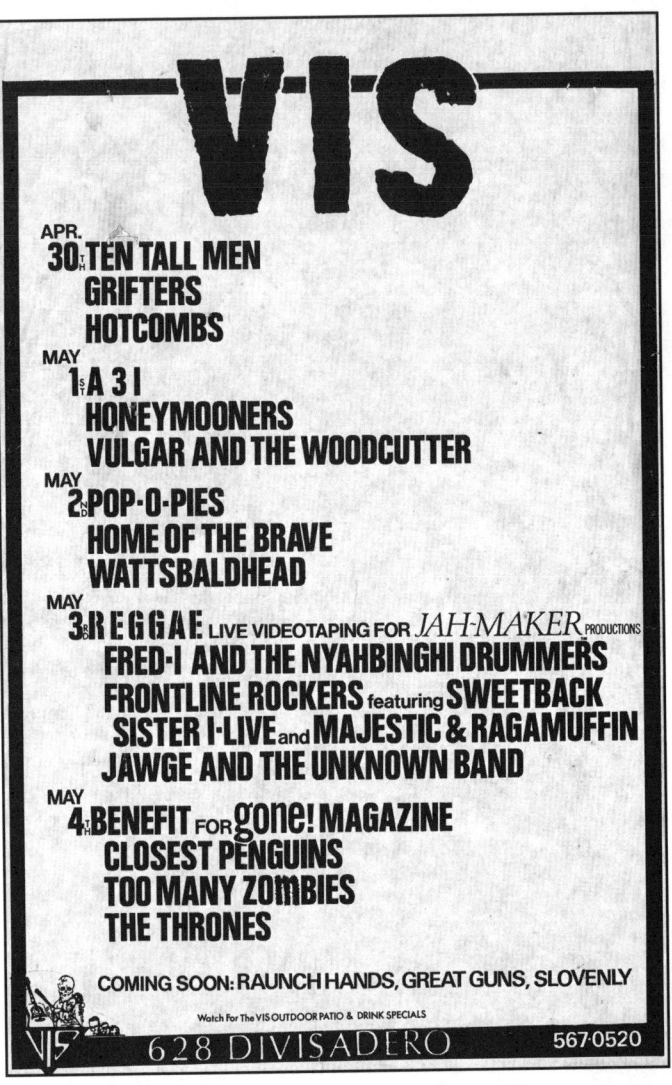

SPECIAL FUN

16th NOTE
13 FRIDAY DEC.

3160 16th St. San Francisco 621-1617

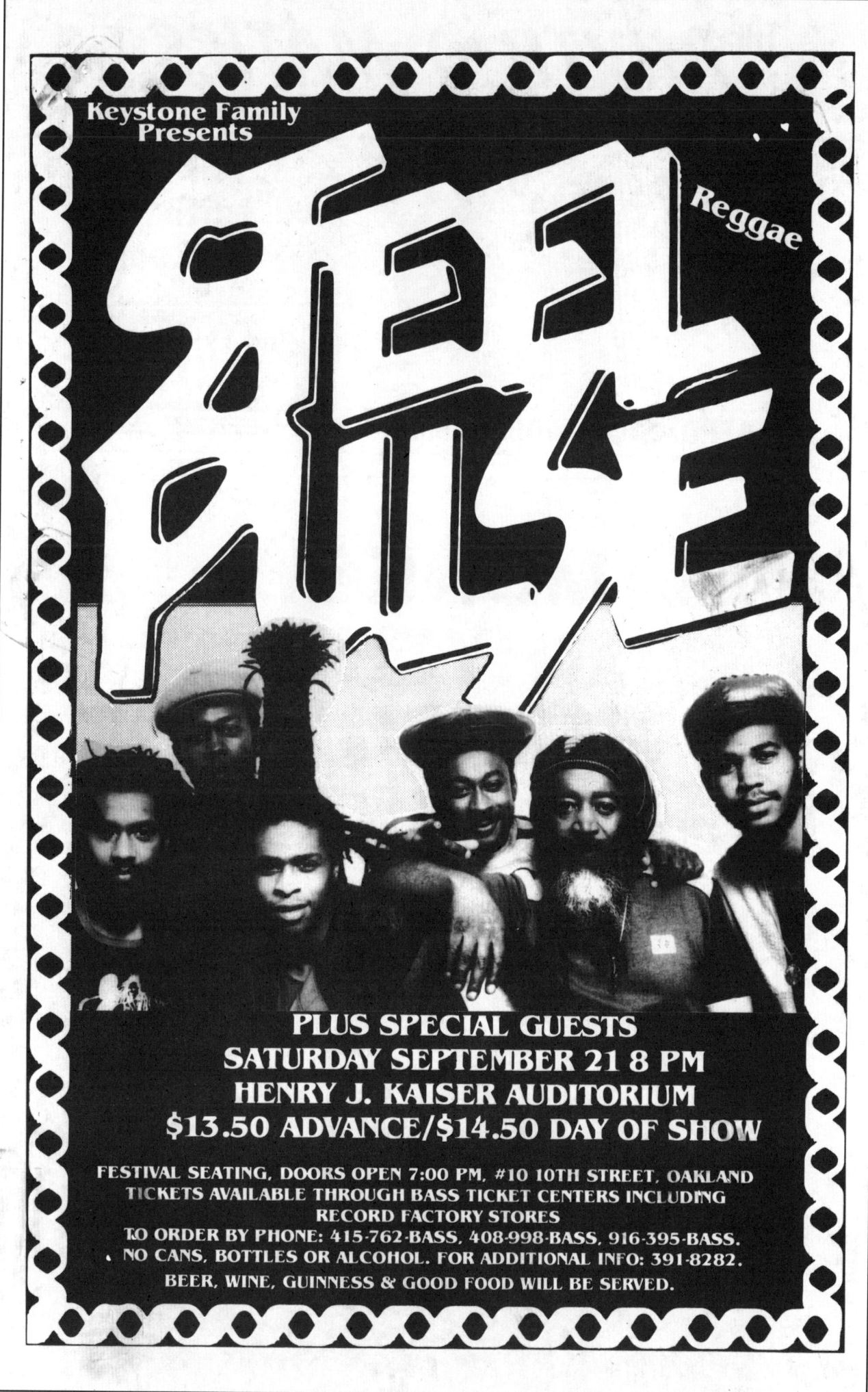

MONKEY RHYTHM

AT

STONE S.F.

WITH

FISHBONE FRI SEPT. 6

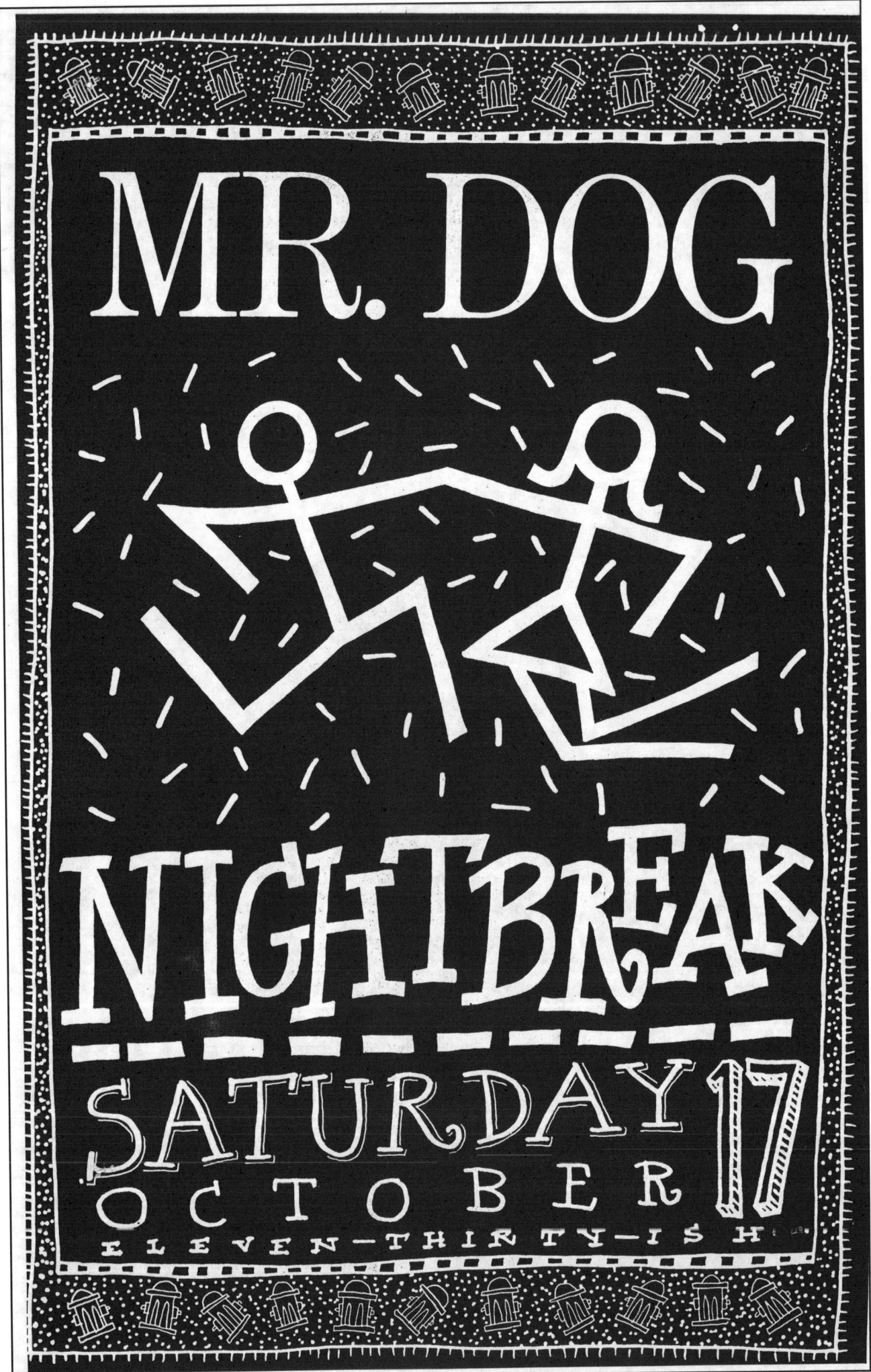

Band Index

A Band Called Horse, 53
Air Tight Garage, 59
Al Rapone, 165
Alpha Blondie, 52
AMC, 10, 161
American English, 217
American Music Club, 55, 84, 196, 251
Animal Slaves, 56
Anne Earthling And The Planets, 90, 95
Anson and the Rockets with Sam Myers, 83
Archipelago Brewing Co., 23, 47, 251
Arlo Guthrie, 157
Arsenal, 36
Ash Wednesday, 30
Ashwin Batish, 151
Aswad, 160
Autonomy, 26
Bad Dog, 192
Bad Habit, 71
Balancing Act, 17
Baldo Rex, 50, 71, 194
Ballistic Missles, 196
Balphazar, 54
Bandaleers, 123
Bardo, 15, 50, 57, 77, 93, 210
Barking Spiders, 80s, 202
Barry Melton-Spencer Dryden And Friends, 69
Batucaje Samba, 65
Batucaje, 225
Bay Area Rapid Brass, 157
Bead Happening, 11
Beat Club, 73
Beat Farmers, The, 179
Beat Freaks, 57, 140
Beat Girl, 68, 76, 167, 181
Beatnigs, The, 57, 58, 104, 108, 109, 110, 221, 251
Beatnik Beatch, 213
Beauty of Dogs, 166
Beloved, 51, 193
Benjamin Bossi, 133
Bhundu Boys, 63
Big City and The Looters, 216
Big City, 83, 87, 91, 131, 135, 166, 201
Big Dipper, 178
Big House, 81
Big Pig, 43
Big Voice, 131
Big Wheel, The, 71, 91, 237
Big Youth and The Ark Angels, 147
Birdkillers, 81, 111, 114, 140, 184, 243

Black Athletes, 124, 136, 153, 163, 171
Black Circus, 53
Black Emotion, 68, 76
Black Majic Rydim Rockers, The, 19
Black Swans, The, 18
Blackberri, 153
Blacklight Chameleons, 20
Bliss Boy Perez, 10
Block 15, 219
Bloco De Amigos, 106
Blue Movie, 15, 46, 122, 185, 194
Blue Riddum Band, 181
Blue Stucco, 37
Board of Mackeral, 30
Bob Darlington, 213
Bob Gibson, 145, 218
Bob Pryor, 140
Boby Baino, 141
Bohemian Luv Jones, 86, 193, 196, 220
Bolshoi, 128
Bolt, 6, 175
Bomber Bomber Bomber, 97, 105
Bonedaddys, 140
Boneyard, 55
Boomer, 22, 31
Boots, 69
Borman 6, 108, 151
Boss Hoss, 9, 62, 188
Boxing Factory, 110
Brian Raffi Red Square, 229
Bridge, 167
Bringdowns, 50
Buck Naked and the Bare Bottom Boys, 164, 185
Buffalo Roam, 64, 75, 88
Bunny Drums, 179
Burlezk, 36
Burning Spear, 167
Buzz in the System, 14
Bwana Devils, 188
Byrd Hale, 83
Cabaret Method, 14
Caffe Latte, 115
Call Me Bwana, 50
Calling, The, 40, 212
Camper Van Beethoven, 21, 56, 86, 89, 109, 136, 151
Capture the Flag, 53, 136, 204, 211
Caribbean Allstars, 25, 61, 174, 177, 228
Carnial Law, 50
Carolina, 50
Casselberry and DuPree, 218
Casual Italians, 41

Catheads, 15, 96, 162, 207, 243
Chameleons, The, 102
Change, 53
Changling, 71
Chaos, 40
Charlie Haden, 158
Chris Cain Band, 24, 25
Cindy, 197
City of Industry, 204
Clark Taylor, 10
Class, The, 70, 91, 223
Comic Book Opera, 51, 126
Confessions, 15
Congo Phil, 68, 202
Conjunto Cespedes, 60, 102
Convictions, 120, 122
Covergirls, 218
Crash Puppies, 120
Crawl Away Machine, 4, 62
Crazy 8s, 178
Cricket Men, 172
Crucial Youth, 61
Cultural Odyssey, 219
Curtis Salgado, 83
Cycle Soul Blues, 133
D Bs, The, 17
D.J Tony Corben, 246
D.J. Adam Fisher, 20
D.J. Doug Wendt and The Midnight Dread Sight and Sound System, 24, 25
D.J. Ekemode and The Nigerian Allstars, 120
D.J. Shea & Essen, 18
Dash Rip Rock, 204
Davenports, 188
David Lindley, 52
David Merrill, 133
David Pirner, 164
Dawson Tate, 42
DC3, 76
Deadbeats, The, 58
Debbie Saunders, 66
Debora Marta, 28
Deborah Iyall and The Lower East Venus, 136
Deborah Iyall, 53, 114
Dee Russell and The Bags, 50
Defectors, 147
Dega-Ray, 11
Denim TV, 75, 241
Diamanda Galas, 208
Diane and The Nutron Dancers, 97
Die Bossa Nova, 14, 76
DiFi, 75
Dinos, The, 217
DNZ, 197

Dodgy Boilers, 46
Dog Talk, 214
Don and Handbone, 140
Don Murphy, 164
Dot 3, 214
Dottie Ivory, 240
Doug Hamblin / Jan Fanucci Band, 24
Dread at the Controls, 239
Dressed To Kill, 38
Dumptruck, 158
DV8, 197
Dynatones, 14
East Bay Ray, 140
Ebony, 35
Eddie And The Tide, 159
Eddie Cockring, 217
Eddie Ray Porter, 17
88 Magik, 46
El Rayo-x, 52
Elbows Akimbo, 26
Electric Piece, 210
Elliot Schneider, 84
Emerald Web, 157
Epidemics, 159
Eskimo, 6, 44, 50, 194
Eugene and The Blue Genes, 78
Eugene Chadbourne, 47
Expose, 118
Faces of Drama, 51
Faith Museum, 110
Faith No More, 5, 11, 17, 98, 170, 210, 251
Faye Spain, 80
Fela, 143
Ferron and The Shadows on the Dime Band, 157
Fifth Business, 202
54.40, 109
Fillmore 4, 15, 46, 210
Fillmore House, 198
Fire Mission, 67, 134
Firehose, 76, 109
Fishbone, 130, 211
Flowers at Night, 193
Flying Color, 7, 133
4-Way Cross, 188
Freaky Executives, The, 81, 114, 117, 120, 137, 144, 146, 150, 159, 174, 197, 235
Fred I and the Nyahbinghi Drummers, 242
Frightwig, 136, 140
Frontier Wives, 50, 178, 204, 252
Frontline Rockers, 9, 239
Fua Dia Congo Drummers, 225
Fuasis, 156

Fuck Bubble, 150
Funkee Fresh Posse, 18
Funky Fresh Crew, 117
Funky Town, 211
Furies, The, 15
G T Jesus and the Crawling Asylum, 4
Game Theory, 179
Gary Smith Blues Band, 240
Gary Smith, 83
Girl Can't Help It, 236
Glorious Din, 11, 126, 210
Going To Pieces, 215
Gone World, 29, 84
Gordon Gang, 109
Gotta Wanna, 130
Great Divide, 122
Green Onions, 69
Green River, 9
Greg Gumbel and Friends, 53
Grey Matter, 211
Grupo Cultural, 147
Guadalcanal Diary, 85, 162
Gunga Din, 45
Gwen Avery, 66, 173
Gwen Avery Show, The, 36
Gwen Majors, 251
Harry's Picket Fence, 251
Havana 3:00 AM, 178
Heart Beat, 122
Heru Ra Ha, 71
Hitchhikers, The, 53
Hi-Tech, 91
Holly Near, 157
Holy Sisters of the Gaga Dada, 183
House of Freaks, 81, 152, 158, 178
House of Wheels, 14, 71
Housecoat Project, 22
Hut Hut, 157
Hydro-Matics, 40
Hysteric Narcotics, 183
I Claudine, 228
Impatient Youth, 77
Imperialist, 69
Impulse F, 99, 246
Infant Bonds of Joy, 184
Inkspots, 6
Inner City, 52
Intergalactic Funketeers, 79
Inti Illimani, 157
J.C. Hopkins, 50, 188
Jah Big, 177, 228
Jah Big and the Steppin Razor Band, 52
Jah Wize, 18
Jain, 159
Javahar, 93
Jazzy E and Mighty Mouth, 117
Jeffrey Lee Pierce, 123
Jeffery Lee Pierce Quartet, The, 102
Jerry McCain, 83
Jerry Shelfer, 51
Jimmy Cliff, 52
Joady Guthry, 84
Joe Dudley and Co., 10
Joe Ely, 81
Joe Louis Walker and The Boss Talkers, 14
Joe Mama, 86, 123, 123, 204
John Belushi Memorial Blues Band, The, 57
John Cale and Chris Spedding, 213
John Handy, 228
Johnny and The Chips, 202
Joni Haastrup, 90, 93, 117, 143
Jr. Walker and The Allstars, 25
Judy Small, 157
Jungle Book, 11
Jungle Studs, 17, 98, 184
K C Mattax the Blues Doctor, 10
Kage, The, 191
Kamikaze Ground Crew, 217
Karmakanix, 213
Kate Wolf, 157
Keith Gayle Band, 182
Key, The, 58
Kill The Messenger, 23
Kimathi Asante, 32
King Sunny Ade, 143
Kooch Behar, 98
Kotoja, 57, 213
Ku Ku Ku, 170, 210
Kukaudu, 120
Lady Margaret, 35
Lambsbread, 28, 177
Latin Allstars Band, 28
Lauren, 211
Lawn Vultures, 14, 217
Lazy Lester, 83
Leather Nun, The, 44
Legal Reins, 85, 140, 144, 202, 210
Les Rita Mitsouko, 48
Life of the Party, 9
Lil' Ed and The Blues Imperials, 24
Limbo Maniacs, 115, 135, 211, 217
Linda Tillery, 157
Little Charlie and the Nightcats, 14, 24, 83
Little Women, 52
Live Skull, 170
Living in a Dream, 211
Looters, The, 37, 49, 94, 100, 187, 102, 109, 139, 140, 209, 213, 216
Lords of the New Church, 62
Los Microwaves, 93
Love Club, 76, 128, 188, 196
Lower East Venus, 53, 114
M-1 Alternative, 14, 27, 121, 132, 140, 154
M-1 Harmony, 133
Mad Hatters, 53
Malopoets, The, 69
Man from Missouri, 98
Mapenzi, 35, 39, 83, 83, 95, 117, 143, 148, 149, 153, 159, 181, 202, 231, 232
Mark Hummel and The Blues Survivors, 211
Marty Balin, 157n, 159
Marylin Taxi, 14
Matica, 147, 187
Maurice Mckinnies and The Electrifying Galaxy II Band, 54
Maximillions M.C., 196
MC Casanova L.B., 117
Mcguires, 50
Mchael X, 134
MCM and the Monster, 57, 103, 115, 123, 123, 164, 172
MC. Tony Moses, 147
Mechanical Bride, 126
Meditations, 79
Mercy Seat, 109
M-Fakter, 243
Michael Bolivar, 157
Might Lemondrops, The, 102
Mighty Diamonds, The, 107
Mighty Diamonds and The Diamonds Band, 63
Mighty Fliers with Rod Piazza, 83
Mikey Dread, 239
Miles Long, 31
Minimal Man, 36
Mint Julep, 11
Miracle Legion, 152
Miss Kitty, 33, 86
Missile Harmony, 37, 116, 121, 133, 165, 203
Mississippi Johnny Waters, 211
Mix, The, 157
Mod Mach, 124
Moit Moit, 22
Mojo, 93, 114, 166
Mon-kee Rid-um, 62
Monkey Rhythm, 52, 59, 62, 126, 137, 180, 189, 212, 224, 248
Monks of Doom, 57
Monty Hoffman, 133
Moon Club, 106
Moonball Express, 198
Morris Tepper, 10
Motophonics, 12
Movement Underground, 50
Mr Hyde, 98
Mr. Dog, 133, 151, 213, 250
Mr. T Experience, 14
Mrs Green, 7, 8, 16, 19, 34, 114, 136, 169, 227
Mud Dogs, The, 190
Murmers, 130
Muskrats The, 109, 145, 218
Mutabaruka and The Sounds of Resistance, 24
Muvies, The, 69
Muyei Africa, 176
Mysteries, The, 53, 200
Mystic Youth, 57
Naked Into, The, 10, 42, 55, 72, 84, 104, 162, 179, 196, 211
Nancie De Ross, 141
Nancy De Ross, 118
Natives, The, 53
Necropolis of Love, 153
Negative Trend, 11
Neighborhoods The, 213
Neon, 111
New Breed, 166, 207
New Deal Rhythm Band, 92
New Ice Age, The, 94
New Model Army, 4
Next To Nothin, 36
Nice Guys, 178, 252
Nigerian Allstars, 231,232
Nip Drivers, 118
No Grenades, 183
Nonfiction, 13, 22, 75, 122
Noon Day Underground, 166
Norman Salant, 133
Norton Buffalo, 157
Nova Mob, The, 31, 66, 76, 98, 121, 136, 181, 184, 222, 246
NRBQ, 217
NYN, 194
O.J. Ekemode, 231, 232
Oblong Rhonda, 86, 151, 181, 246
Obo Addy, 120
Offs, 77
Ogie Yocha, 9, 177, 192
One Take Jake, 103, 113
Opal, 151, 197
Ophelias, The, 89, 116, 197
Orange Curtain, 152, 180
Pablo Moses and Jah Kingdom, 63
Palmetto State, 75
Pamela Z, 11
Panther Burns, 220
Papa Stretch, 18
Paranoid Blue, 194
Paris Slim, 240
Party Naked, 4
Party of Five, 196
Pat Wilder, 66
Ped Xing, 199
Ped Z Ing, 50
Pee Wee Crayton, 240
Pennsylvania Mahoney and her Safe Sextet, 74
Perry Smith Band, 35
Peter Apfelbaum and the Hieroglyphics Ensemble, 63
Philip Dimitri Galas, 14
Phranc, 145, 218
PianoSaurus, 181
Piglatin, 30, 74, 104, 141, 170
Pirates of Venus, 111
Poison 13, 4
Polkacide, 136
Pop On Trial, 71
Pray For Rain, 7, 51, 53, 196, 211
Pre Fix, 36
Pride And Joy, 34, 150
Primus, 217
Prince Ital Joe, 233
Prince Joni and The Beat, 90
Prince Joni and the World Beat Jam, 143
Princess Bam Bam, 233
Pschefunkapus, 214
Pseudo Echo, 211
Psycho Souls, 33, 86, 196, 217
QT, 130
Rage of Eden, 6
Rain Makers, The, 14
Rain Rust, 11
Ram, 98
Randy X, 47
Rank And File, 13, 77, 109
Rankin Scroo and Ginger, 61
Ras Michael and the Sons of Negus, 233
Ras Michael and The Sons and Daughters of Negus, 107
Ras Smurfin', 18
Raskidus, 233
Ray Charles, 142
R-Complex, 234, 238
Red Devils, 136
Reggae Killer, 9
Reggie and The Rebels, 111
Responsibles, 45, 196
Rhythm and Noise, 249
Rhythm Riot, 251
Rhyth-O Matics, 32, 72, 79, 101, 174, 242, 248
Richard Barone, 178
Richard Howell, 127
Ridim Section, 177, 228
Risk, The, 58
Robert Kelton, 240

Robin Hitchcock and The Egyptians, 138
Rogies Muyei Africa, 69
Romeo Blue, 117
Ron Thomson and The Resistors, 78
Ronnie Gilbert, 157
Rogue Elephant, 171
Roy Buchanan, 24
Ruler Tone High Power, 239
Sachiko, 140
Safe Sex, 71
Samba Ngo, 156
Saqqara Dogs, 76, 99, 125
Savage Republic, 170
Scramblurs, 42
Screamin Sirens, 172, 185
Seahags, The, 5, 76, 98, 136
See Page 2, 223
Selector Chuckie, 239
7 God Damn Girl drummers, 47
700 Club, 188
Sex Farm, 71
Shameless, 14
Shara, 93
Shark Bait, 114, 203
Sharon McNight, 150
She Devils, 196
Shiva Dancing, 15, 71, 89, 126
Short Dogs Grow, 110, 136, 197
Show and Tell, 21, 72
Shower Scene, 50
Shy Hands, 52, 76, 126, 166, 208, 210, 212
Sidewinder, 153
Sister Cheyenne, 228
Sister Double Happiness, 57, 111, 136, 140
Sisters of Zion, 233
Siva Burlesque, 56
Siva Dancing, 103
Skin Trade, 152
Slack, 217
Slantstep, 50, 130
Slovenly, 243
Snapp, The, 86, 91, 103, 196
Snappers, 118
Sneeches, The, 14, 114, 123, 158, 246
Snuky, 11
So…, 72
Solar System, 52
Something Else, 32
Sonic Surgery, 206
Sonic Surgery by D.J.s Desmond Shea And John Essen, 26
Sonny Rollins, 85
Sonya Hunter, 50
Sooliman, 120
Sorentinos, 53
Soul Asylum, 110
Soul Kitchen, 166
Sound Garden, 14
Sound Policy, 75
Spanish Elvis, 48, 89, 103, 205
Spare Parts, 111
Special Forces, 153
Special Fun, 101, 139, 244
Spider Box, 11
Spontanic, 147
Spot 1019, 56, 57, 136, 178, 188, 241, 252
Square Roots, 44, 61, 178
Stand, The, 47
Standing Naked, 16, 76
Steel Pulse, 247
Stick Against Stone, 41, 57, 122, 136, 137, 245
Stick Figures, 82
Strange Angel, 135
Strappado, 122
Strictly Roots, 107, 177
Stupid, 42
Sudden Changes, 127
Sugar Beats, 158
Sundae Knight Banned, 69
Supplicants, 133
Sweet Honey in the Rock, 157
Sweet K and Jerry D, 117
Sweetback, 9
Symphony of Satire, 9, 183
Sync, The, 69
Syncopation, 218
Taiko Dojo Drums, 225
Tambokuba, 225
Tao Mao, 152
Tarumbae And The Rydim Rockers, 177, 218
Ted Czuk, 140
Tekno Fear, 158, 163
Ten Tall Men, 75, 134, 242
10,000 maniacs, 89
Terminators of Endearment, 53, 84
Terra Incognita, 84, 242
Thaddeus, 61
Thin White Rope, 6, 241
Third World, 25
Three Harp Boogie, 83
Thrill of the Pull, 194, 220
Time 2, 9
Toasters, The, 55
Tom Robinson Band, 112
Tommie, 150
Tone Clusters, The, 14
Too Much Fun, 56, 68, 86, 87, 93, 97, 107, 146, 147, 167, 173, 176, 182, 188, 195, 198, 202, 205, 226, 230, 237
Too Short, 113
Tooth and Nail, 14, 72, 76, 89, 98, 128, 133, 136, 165, 191, 235, 251
Toure Kunda, 167
Tragic Mulatto, 30, 150
Translator, 122, 189, 227
Trial, 124
Tricobra, 209
Tripod Jimmie, 170
Trouble Funk, 100
True West, 59, 179
Tunnel Creeps, 136
Tuxedomoon, 121
23 Screams, 126, 210
Two Guys from Gilroy, 252
Typhoon Bomb, 114
Typhoon, 71, 105, 106, 194
Tziganya, 85
Uh-Oh, 36
Ulterior Motives, 40
Ultra Sheen, 77
Undercover, 34
Universal Congress, 210
Unruly World, 21, 55, 209
Until December, 98, 220
Urban Africa, 10
US Girls, 105, 132, 231, 232
Val Serrant and Friends, 177
Vauxhall, 5
Verse, 26
Vicelords, 188
Village Drummers from Trinidad and Tobago, 225
Vipers The, 168
Vision International, 19
Vision, 27, 42, 157, 174, 218
Viv Akauldren, 105, 169
Vivisection, 76, 191
Voice Farm, 86, 93, 144, 151, 155, 181, 246
Voices, 5, 19, 32
Vomit Launch, 150
Voodoo a Go-Go, 202
Vos Do Samba, 185
Wailers, The, 197
Walkabouts The, 183
Wall of Voodoo, 7
Wally Smith, 50
Warriors of the Beat, 226
Washington Squares, The, 145, 218
Watchmen, 164, 204
Whitefronts, 21, 141
Whorl, 21, 118, 122
Wild Brides, 50
William D. Burton, 50
Wiretrain, 53, 99
Witness, 243
Witnesses, The, 50, 77, 147
Woodentops The, 197
World Entertainment War, 198, 203
World War Love, 34
X-Tal, 11
Xymox, 110
Yak Butter, 50
Yanks, 45
YHVH, 242
Yo, 96, 98, 102, 123, 138, 162, 169, 184, 243
Zasu Pitts Memorial Orchestra, 150, 200
Zendiks, 21, 114
Zula Pool, 94, 107, 131, 182, 186, 190, 202, 248
Zulu Spear, 7, 32, 39, 56, 83, 91, 94, 107, 139, 140, 148, 157, 159, 201, 231, 232
Zulu Warriors, 57, 202
Zydeco Express, 165

Club Index

Ashkenaz, 28, 37
Avolation, 194
Baybrick, 36, 50, 66, 75, 103, 187
Baybrick Inn, 204
Berkeley Community Theater, 52
Berkeley Square, 138
Bolt the, 6, 175
Cesars, 140
Cesar's Palace, 28, 228, 233
Chatterbox, 111, 166
Chi Chi Club, 5, 22, 31, 118, 167, 188
Club DV8, 121, 128
Club Foot, 11, 59
Cotati Cabaret, 237
Creative Arts Center, 32
Das Club, 167
Deaf Club, 11
Depot at Mission Rock, 250
DNA Lounge, 20, 34, 76, 108, 114, 119, 133, 136, 140, 237, 242
Dore Alley, 251
El Rio, 27
Farm, The, 7, 32, 114, 117, 120, 122, 124, 127, 136, 140, 177, 187, 209, 211, 216
Fillmore, The, 52
Firehouse 7, 18, 57, 194, 206
520 4th St., 229
Flashback, 205
Fort Mason, 14
4 Mile House, 10
Freight and Salvage, 85
Full Moon Saloon, 8, 21, 34, 35, 36, 40, 41, 42, 55, 56, 57, 64, 68, 70, 75, 78, 82, 86, 87, 88, 90, 91, 95, 96, 105, 107, 111, 114, 137, 146, 158, 174, 182, 196, 212, 235
Galleria, The, 25
Golden Gate park Bandshell, 225
Graffiti, 11
Grandia Room, 73
Great American Music Hall, 83, 93, 94, 101, 148, 158
Greek Theater, 157
Gumption Theater, 10
Henry J. Kaiser Convention Center, 247
Hotel Utah, 46, 75, 77, 150
I-Beam, 4, 5, 7, 13, 17, 38, 43, 48, 55, 56, 57, 76, 81, 85, 86, 89, 91, 93, 94, 98, 100, 102, 109, 110, 123, 151, 158, 173, 179, 181, 185, 197, 200, 201
Jimmies, 132
Kennel Club, The, 10, 14, 24, 25, 30, 49, 53, 57, 61, 63, 72, 98, 103, 109, 140, 152, 165, 170, 178, 181, 197, 211, 213, 217, 220, 243, 252
Keyboard Theater, 6
Keystone, 27, 160
Koncepts, 156
La Pena Cultural Center, 141, 185, 218
Larry Blakes R&B Cafe, 215
Last Day Saloon, 107, 122, , 226
Lipps Underground, 22, 23
Mabuhay Gardens, 45, 58, 71, 75, 147
Major Ponds, 94, 176, 218, 220, 236
Max's, 194
Moon Club, 66
Mortys, 251
Movement Underground, 50
Nightbreak, 6, 7, 27, 33, 34, 37, 41, 42, 44, 46, 47, 50, 51, 53, 54, 56, 58, 59, 62, 68, 72, 76, 81, 86, 89, 91, 98, 99, 103, 104, 105, 107, 108, 110, 113, 115, 116, 121, 123, 125, 126, 133, 136, 141, 152, 154, 161, 164, 168, 169, 179, 180, 182, 183, 184, 185, 186, 190, 191, 193, 196, 204, 205, 212, 221, 224, 235, 238, 246, 250
Nine, 31, 106, 158, 162, 208, 222, 227, 234, 242
Nobody's Inn, 15
Noe Valley Ministry, 11, 217
Oakland Hyatt, 197
Oakland Theater, 107
Oasis, The, 12, 99, 219
Old Fillmore Theater, 83, 232
Omni, The, 120, 130
181 Club, 162
Palace of Fine Arts, 85
Palms, The, 92
Paradise Lounge, 80, 214
Paramount Theater, 142
Purgatory, 4
River Theater, 97
Rose and Thistle, 15
Rouge Elephant, 171
Russian Hall, 79
Ruthies Inn, 205
S.F Music Works, 55, 71, 74, 93
S.F. Art Institute, 147
S.F. Civic Center, 150, 153
S.F. Music Works, 44, 47, 50, 172, 183, 196, 210
Sacred Grounds Cafe, 10
Savoy Tivoli, 36
16th Note, 16, 19, 26, 29, 39, 42, 55, 60, 65, 68, 84, 93, 106, 133, 147, 149, 163, 173, 194, 195, 198, 199, 202, 207, 208, 230, 244, 248
Software, 35, 54, 251
Sonoma Co. Fairgrounds, 157, 159
Sound of Music, 67, 134
Starry Plough, 21, 53, 69
Stone, The, 6, 21, 52, 61, 62, 69, 81, 89, 122, 126, 131, 137, 143, 146, 160, 162, 166, 167, 170, 174, 189, 211, 248
Swedish Music Hall, 4
10th St. Hall, 77
Trocadero Transfer, 246
Trocadero, 105, 132, 231
Trude Heller, 194
Uncle Charlie's, 40
Underground, 132
Versus, 198, 203
Vesuvio Cafe, 67
Victoria Theater, 240
Vincenzo's, 202
Vis, The, 9, 14, 15, 118, 126, 130, 170, 185, 188, 192, 208, 210, 223, 227, 239, 241, 242, 243, 246
Warehouse Restaurant, 155
Wheeler Auditorium, 145
Wheeler Stadium, 218
Wolfgang's, 63, 123, 129, 133, 135, 139, 144, 210
Zellerbach Auditorium, 112